Learning Apache Kafka

Second Edition

Start from scratch and learn how to administer Apache Kafka effectively for messaging

Nishant Garg

BIRMINGHAM - MUMBAI

Learning Apache Kafka
Second Edition

First published: October 2013

Second edition: February 2015

Production reference: 1210215

Published by Packt Publishing Ltd.
Livery Place
35 Livery Street
Birmingham B3 2PB, UK.

ISBN 978-1-78439-309-0

www.packtpub.com

Credits

Author
Nishant Garg

Reviewers
Sandeep Khurana

Saurabh Minni

Supreet Sethi

Commissioning Editor
Usha Iyer

Acquisition Editor
Meeta Rajani

Content Development Editor
Shubhangi Dhamgaye

Technical Editors
Manal Pednekar

Chinmay S. Puranik

Copy Editors
Merilyn Pereira

Aarti Saldanha

Project Coordinator
Harshal Ved

Proofreaders
Stephen Copestake

Paul Hindle

Indexer
Rekha Nair

Graphics
Sheetal Aute

Production Coordinator
Nilesh R. Mohite

Cover Work
Nilesh R. Mohite

About the Author

Nishant Garg has over 14 years of software architecture and development experience in various technologies, such as Java Enterprise Edition, SOA, Spring, Hadoop, Hive, Flume, Sqoop, Oozie, Spark, Shark, YARN, Impala, Kafka, Storm, Solr/Lucene, NoSQL databases (such as HBase, Cassandra, and MongoDB), and MPP databases (such as GreenPlum).

He received his MS in software systems from the Birla Institute of Technology and Science, Pilani, India, and is currently working as a technical architect for the Big Data R&D Group with Impetus Infotech Pvt. Ltd. Previously, Nishant has enjoyed working with some of the most recognizable names in IT services and financial industries, employing full software life cycle methodologies such as Agile and SCRUM.

Nishant has also undertaken many speaking engagements on big data technologies and is also the author of *HBase Essestials*, *Packt Publishing*.

I would like to thank my parents (Mr. Vishnu Murti Garg and Mrs. Vimla Garg) for their continuous encouragement and motivation throughout my life. I would also like to thank my wife (Himani) and my kids (Nitigya and Darsh) for their never-ending support, which keeps me going.

Finally, I would like to thank Vineet Tyagi, CTO and Head of Innovation Labs, Impetus, and Dr. Vijay, Director of Technology, Innovation Labs, Impetus, for encouraging me to write.

About the Reviewers

Sandeep Khurana, an 18 years veteran, comes with an extensive experience in the Software and IT industry. Being an early entrant in the domain, he has worked in all aspects of Java- / JEE-based technologies and frameworks such as Spring, Hibernate, JPA, EJB, security, Struts, and so on. For the last few professional engagements in his career and also partly due to his personal interest in consumer-facing analytics, he has been treading in the big data realm and has extensive experience on big data technologies such as Hadoop, Pig, Hive, ZooKeeper, Flume, Oozie, HBase and so on.

He has designed, developed, and delivered multiple enterprise-level, highly scalable, distributed systems during the course of his career. In his long and fruitful professional life, he has been with some of the biggest names of the industry such as IBM, Oracle, Yahoo!, and Nokia.

Saurabh Minni is currently working as a technical architect at AdNear. He completed his BE in computer science at the Global Academy of Technology, Bangalore. He is passionate about programming and loves getting his hands wet with different technologies.

At AdNear, he deployed Kafka. This enabled smooth consumption of data to be processed by Storm and Hadoop clusters. Prior to AdNear, he worked with Adobe and Intuit, where he dabbled with C++, Delphi, Android, and Java while working on desktop and mobile products.

Supreet Sethi is a seasoned technology leader with an eye for detail. He has proven expertise in charting out growth strategies for technology platforms. He currently steers the platform team to create tools that drive the infrastructure at Jabong. He often reviews the code base from a performance point of view. These aspects also put him at the helm of backend systems, APIs that drive mobile apps, mobile web apps, and desktop sites.

The Jabong tech team has been extremely helpful during the review process. They provided a creative environment where Supreet was able to explore some of cutting-edge technologies like Apache Kafka.

I would like to thank my daughter, Seher, and my wife, Smriti, for being patient observers while I spent a few hours everyday reviewing this book.

www.PacktPub.com

Support files, eBooks, discount offers, and more

For support files and downloads related to your book, please visit www.PacktPub.com.

Did you know that Packt offers eBook versions of every book published, with PDF and ePub files available? You can upgrade to the eBook version at www.PacktPub.com and as a print book customer, you are entitled to a discount on the eBook copy. Get in touch with us at service@packtpub.com for more details.

At www.PacktPub.com, you can also read a collection of free technical articles, sign up for a range of free newsletters and receive exclusive discounts and offers on Packt books and eBooks.

https://www2.packtpub.com/books/subscription/packtlib

Do you need instant solutions to your IT questions? PacktLib is Packt's online digital book library. Here, you can search, access, and read Packt's entire library of books.

Why subscribe?

- Fully searchable across every book published by Packt
- Copy and paste, print, and bookmark content
- On demand and accessible via a web browser

Free access for Packt account holders

If you have an account with Packt at www.PacktPub.com, you can use this to access PacktLib today and view 9 entirely free books. Simply use your login credentials for immediate access.

Table of Contents

Preface

This book is here to help you get familiar with Apache Kafka and to solve your challenges related to the consumption of millions of messages in publisher-subscriber architectures. It is aimed at getting you started programming with Kafka so that you will have a solid foundation to dive deep into different types of implementations and integrations for Kafka producers and consumers.

In addition to an explanation of Apache Kafka, we also spend a chapter exploring Kafka integration with other technologies such as Apache Hadoop and Apache Storm. Our goal is to give you an understanding not just of what Apache Kafka is, but also how to use it as a part of your broader technical infrastructure. In the end, we will walk you through operationalizing Kafka where we will also talk about administration.

What this book covers

Chapter 1, Introducing Kafka, discusses how organizations are realizing the real value of data and evolving the mechanism of collecting and processing it. It also describes how to install and build Kafka 0.8.x using different versions of Scala.

Chapter 2, Setting Up a Kafka Cluster, describes the steps required to set up a single- or multi-broker Kafka cluster and shares the Kafka broker properties list.

Chapter 3, Kafka Design, discusses the design concepts used to build the solid foundation for Kafka. It also talks about how Kafka handles message compression and replication in detail.

Chapter 4, Writing Producers, provides detailed information about how to write basic producers and some advanced level Java producers that use message partitioning.

Chapter 5, Writing Consumers, provides detailed information about how to write basic consumers and some advanced level Java consumers that consume messages from the partitions.

Chapter 6, Kafka Integrations, provides a short introduction to both Storm and Hadoop and discusses how Kafka integration works for both Storm and Hadoop to address real-time and batch processing needs.

Chapter 7, Operationalizing Kafka, describes information about the Kafka tools required for cluster administration and cluster mirroring and also shares information about how to integrate Kafka with Camus, Apache Camel, Amazon Cloud, and so on.

What you need for this book

In the simplest case, a single Linux-based (CentOS 6.x) machine with JDK 1.6 installed will give a platform to explore almost all the exercises in this book. We assume you are familiar with command line Linux, so any modern distribution will suffice.

Some of the examples need multiple machines to see things working, so you will require access to at least three such hosts; virtual machines are fine for learning and exploration.

As we also discuss the big data technologies such as Hadoop and Storm, you will generally need a place to run your Hadoop and Storm clusters.

Who this book is for

This book is for those who want to know about Apache Kafka at a hands-on level; the key audience is those with software development experience but no prior exposure to Apache Kafka or similar technologies.

This book is also for enterprise application developers and big data enthusiasts who have worked with other publisher-subscriber-based systems and now want to explore Apache Kafka as a futuristic scalable solution.

Conventions

In this book, you will find a number of styles of text that distinguish between different kinds of information. Here are some examples of these styles, and an explanation of their meaning.

Code words in text are shown as follows: "Download the `jdk-7u67-linux-x64.rpm` release from Oracle's website."

A block of code is set as follows:

```
String messageStr = new String("Hello from Java Producer");
KeyedMessage<Integer, String> data = new KeyedMessage<Integer,
String>(topic, messageStr);
producer.send(data);
```

When we wish to draw your attention to a particular part of a code block, the relevant lines or items are set in bold:

```
Properties props = new Properties();
props.put("metadata.broker.list","localhost:9092");
props.put("serializer.class","kafka.serializer.StringEncoder");
props.put("request.required.acks", "1");
ProducerConfig config = new ProducerConfig(props);
Producer<Integer, String> producer = new Producer<Integer,
    String>(config);
```

Any command line input or output is written as follows:

```
[root@localhost kafka-0.8]# java SimpleProducer kafkatopic Hello_There
```

New terms and **important words** are shown in bold.

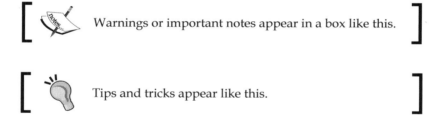

Warnings or important notes appear in a box like this.

Tips and tricks appear like this.

Reader feedback

Feedback from our readers is always welcome. Let us know what you think about this book—what you liked or may have disliked. Reader feedback is important for us to develop titles that you really get the most out of.

To send us general feedback, simply send an e-mail to feedback@packtpub.com, and mention the book title via the subject of your message.

If there is a topic that you have expertise in and you are interested in either writing or contributing to a book, see our author guide on www.packtpub.com/authors.

Customer support

Now that you are the proud owner of a Packt book, we have a number of things to help you to get the most from your purchase.

Errata

Although we have taken every care to ensure the accuracy of our content, mistakes do happen. If you find a mistake in one of our books—maybe a mistake in the text or the code—we would be grateful if you would report this to us. By doing so, you can save other readers from frustration and help us improve subsequent versions of this book. If you find any errata, please report them by visiting http://www.packtpub.com/submit-errata, selecting your book, clicking on the **errata submission form** link, and entering the details of your errata. Once your errata are verified, your submission will be accepted and the errata will be uploaded on our website, or added to any list of existing errata, under the Errata section of that title. Any existing errata can be viewed by selecting your title from http://www.packtpub.com/support.

Piracy

Piracy of copyright material on the Internet is an ongoing problem across all media. At Packt, we take the protection of our copyright and licenses very seriously. If you come across any illegal copies of our works, in any form, on the Internet, please provide us with the location address or website name immediately so that we can pursue a remedy.

Please contact us at copyright@packtpub.com with a link to the suspected pirated material.

We appreciate your help in protecting our authors, and our ability to bring you valuable content.

Questions

You can contact us at questions@packtpub.com if you are having a problem with any aspect of the book, and we will do our best to address it.

1
Introducing Kafka

In today's world, real-time information is continuously being generated by applications (business, social, or any other type), and this information needs easy ways to be reliably and quickly routed to multiple types of receivers. Most of the time, applications that produce information and applications that are consuming this information are well apart and inaccessible to each other. These heterogeneous application leads to redevelopment for providing an integration point between them. Therefore, a mechanism is required for the seamless integration of information from producers and consumers to avoid any kind of application rewriting at either end.

Welcome to the world of Apache Kafka

In the present big-data era, the very first challenge is to collect the data as it is a huge amount of data and the second challenge is to analyze it. This analysis typically includes the following types of data and much more:

- User behavior data
- Application performance tracing
- Activity data in the form of logs
- Event messages

Message publishing is a mechanism for connecting various applications with the help of messages that are routed between—for example, by a message broker such as Kafka. Kafka is a solution to the real-time problems of any software solution; that is to say, dealing with real-time volumes of information and routing it to multiple consumers quickly. Kafka provides seamless integration between information from producers and consumers without blocking the producers of the information and without letting producers know who the final consumers are.

Apache Kafka is an open source, distributed, partitioned, and replicated commit-log-based publish-subscribe messaging system, mainly designed with the following characteristics:

- **Persistent messaging**: To derive the real value from big data, any kind of information loss cannot be afforded. Apache Kafka is designed with $O(1)$ disk structures that provide constant-time performance even with very large volumes of stored messages that are in the order of TBs. With Kafka, messages are persisted on disk as well as replicated within the cluster to prevent data loss.

- **High throughput**: Keeping big data in mind, Kafka is designed to work on commodity hardware and to handle hundreds of MBs of reads and writes per second from large number of clients.

- **Distributed**: Apache Kafka with its cluster-centric design explicitly supports message partitioning over Kafka servers and distributing consumption over a cluster of consumer machines while maintaining per-partition ordering semantics. Kafka cluster can grow elastically and transparently without any downtime.

- **Multiple client support**: The Apache Kafka system supports easy integration of clients from different platforms such as Java, .NET, PHP, Ruby, and Python.

- **Real time**: Messages produced by the producer threads should be immediately visible to consumer threads; this feature is critical to event-based systems such as **Complex Event Processing (CEP)** systems.

Kafka provides a real-time publish-subscribe solution that overcomes the challenges of consuming the real-time and batch data volumes that may grow in order of magnitude to be larger than the real data. Kafka also supports parallel data loading in the Hadoop systems.

The following diagram shows a typical big data aggregation-and-analysis scenario supported by the Apache Kafka messaging system:

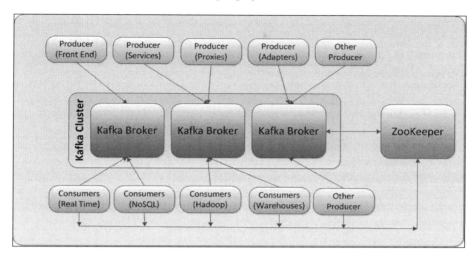

On the production side, there are different kinds of producers, such as the following:

- Frontend web applications generating application logs
- Producer proxies generating web analytics logs
- Producer adapters generating transformation logs
- Producer services generating invocation trace logs

On the consumption side, there are different kinds of consumers, such as the following:

- Offline consumers that are consuming messages and storing them in Hadoop or traditional data warehouse for offline analysis
- Near real-time consumers that are consuming messages and storing them in any NoSQL datastore, such as HBase or Cassandra, for near real-time analytics
- Real-time consumers, such as Spark or Storm, that filter messages in-memory and trigger alert events for related groups

Why do we need Kafka?

A large amount of data is generated by companies having any form of web- or device-based presence and activity. Data is one of the newer ingredients in these Internet-based systems and typically includes user activity; events corresponding to logins; page visits; clicks; social networking activities such as likes, shares, and comments; and operational and system metrics. This data is typically handled by logging and traditional log aggregation solutions due to high throughput (millions of messages per second). These traditional solutions are the viable solutions for providing logging data to an offline analysis system such as Hadoop. However, the solutions are very limiting for building real-time processing systems.

According to the new trends in Internet applications, activity data has become a part of production data and is used to run analytics in real time. These analytics can be:

- Search-based on relevance
- Recommendations based on popularity, co-occurrence, or sentimental analysis
- Delivering advertisements to the masses
- Internet application security from spam or unauthorized data scraping
- Device sensors sending high-temperature alerts
- Any abnormal user behavior or application hacking

Real-time usage of these multiple sets of data collected from production systems has become a challenge because of the volume of data collected and processed.

Apache Kafka aims to unify offline and online processing by providing a mechanism for parallel load in Hadoop systems as well as the ability to partition real-time consumption over a cluster of machines. Kafka can be compared with Scribe or Flume as it is useful for processing activity stream data; but from the architecture perspective, it is closer to traditional messaging systems such as ActiveMQ or RabitMQ.

Kafka use cases

There are number of ways in which Kafka can be used in any architecture. This section discusses some of the popular use cases for Apache Kafka and the well-known companies that have adopted Kafka. The following are the popular Kafka use cases:

- **Log aggregation**: This is the process of collecting physical log files from servers and putting them in a central place (a file server or HDFS) for processing. Using Kafka provides clean abstraction of log or event data as a stream of messages, thus taking away any dependency over file details. This also gives lower-latency processing and support for multiple data sources and distributed data consumption.

- **Stream processing**: Kafka can be used for the use case where collected data undergoes processing at multiple stages—an example is raw data consumed from topics and enriched or transformed into new Kafka topics for further consumption. Hence, such processing is also called stream processing.

- **Commit logs**: Kafka can be used to represent external commit logs for any large scale distributed system. Replicated logs over Kafka cluster help failed nodes to recover their states.

- **Click stream tracking**: Another very important use case for Kafka is to capture user click stream data such as page views, searches, and so on as real-time publish-subscribe feeds. This data is published to central topics with one topic per activity type as the volume of the data is very high. These topics are available for subscription, by many consumers for a wide range of applications including real-time processing and monitoring.

- **Messaging**: Message brokers are used for decoupling data processing from data producers. Kafka can replace many popular message brokers as it offers better throughput, built-in partitioning, replication, and fault-tolerance.

Some of the companies that are using Apache Kafka in their respective use cases are as follows:

- **LinkedIn** (www.linkedin.com): Apache Kafka is used at LinkedIn for the streaming of activity data and operational metrics. This data powers various products such as LinkedIn News Feed and LinkedIn Today, in addition to offline analytics systems such as Hadoop.

- **DataSift** (www.datasift.com): At DataSift, Kafka is used as a collector to monitor events and as a tracker of users' consumption of data streams in real time.

- **Twitter** (www.twitter.com): Twitter uses Kafka as a part of its Storm—a stream-processing infrastructure.

- **Foursquare** (www.foursquare.com): Kafka powers online-to-online and online-to-offline messaging at Foursquare. It is used to integrate Foursquare monitoring and production systems with Foursquare-and Hadoop-based offline infrastructures.

- **Square** (www.squareup.com): Square uses Kafka as a *bus* to move all system events through Square's various datacenters. This includes metrics, logs, custom events, and so on. On the consumer side, it outputs into Splunk, Graphite, or Esper-like real-time alerting.

 The source of the preceding information is https://cwiki.apache.org/confluence/display/KAFKA/Powered+By.

Installing Kafka

Kafka is an Apache project and its current version 0.8.1.1 is available as a stable release. This Kafka 0.8.x offers many advanced features compared to the older version (prior to 0.8.x). A few of its advancements are as follows:

- Prior to 0.8.x, any unconsumed partition of data within the topic could be lost if the broker failed. Now the partitions are provided with a replication factor. This ensures that any committed message would not be lost, as at least one replica is available.

- The previous feature also ensures that all the producers and consumers are replication-aware (the replication factor is a configurable property). By default, the producer's message sending request is blocked until the message is committed to all active replicas; however, producers can also be configured to commit messages to a single broker.

- Like Kafka producers, the Kafka consumer polling model changes to a long-pulling model and gets blocked until a committed message is available from the producer, which avoids frequent pulling.

- Additionally, Kafka 0.8.x also comes with a set of administrative tools, such as controlled cluster shutdown and the Lead replica election tool, for managing the Kafka cluster.

The major limitation with Kafka version 0.8.x is that it can't replace the version prior to 0.8, as it is not backward-compatible.

Coming back to installing Kafka, as a first step we need to download the available stable release (all the processes have been tested on 64-bit CentOS 6.4 OS and may differ on other kernel-based OS). Now let's see what steps need to be followed in order to install Kafka.

Installing prerequisites

Kafka is implemented in Scala and uses build tool **Gradle** to build Kafka binaries. Gradle is a build automation tool for Scala, Groovy, and Java projects that requires Java 1.7 or later.

Installing Java 1.7 or higher

Perform the following steps to install Java 1.7 or later:

1. Download the `jdk-7u67-linux-x64.rpm` release from Oracle's website: http://www.oracle.com/technetwork/java/javase/downloads/index. html.

2. Change the file mode as follows:

```
[root@localhost opt]#chmod +x jdk-7u67-linux-x64.rpm
```

3. Change to the directory in which you want to perform the installation. To do so, type the following command:

```
[root@localhost opt]# cd <directory path name>
```

For example, to install the software in the /usr/java/ directory, type the following command:

```
[root@localhost opt]# cd /usr/java
```

4. Run the installer using the following command:

```
[root@localhost java]# rpm -ivh jdk-7u67-linux-x64.rpm
```

5. Finally, add the environment variable JAVA_HOME. The following command will write the JAVA_HOME environment variable to the file /etc/profile that contains a system-wide environment configuration:

```
[root@localhost opt]# echo "export JAVA_HOME=/usr/java/jdk1.7.0_67
" >> /etc/profile
```

Downloading Kafka

Perform the following steps to download Kafka release 0.8.1.1:

1. Download the current beta release of Kafka (0.8) into a folder on your filesystem (for example, /opt) using the following command:

```
[root@localhost opt]#wget http://apache.tradebit.com/pub/
kafka/0.8.1.1/kafka_2.9.2-0.8.1.1.tgz
```

 The preceding URL may change. Check the correct download version and location at http://kafka.apache.org/downloads.html.

2. Extract the downloaded kafka_2.9.2-0.8.1.1.tgz file using the following command:

```
[root@localhost opt]# tar xzf kafka_2.9.2-0.8.1.1.tgz
```

3. After extraction of the `kafka_2.9.2-0.8.1.1.tgz` file, the directory structure for Kafka 0.8.1.1 looks as follows:

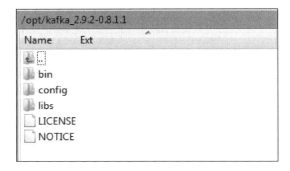

4. Finally, add the Kafka bin folder to PATH as follows:

```
[root@localhost opt]# export KAFKA_HOME=/opt/kafka_2.9.2-0.8.1.1
[root@localhost opt]# export PATH=$PATH:$KAFKA_HOME/bin
```

Building Kafka

The default Scala version that is used to build Kafka release 0.8.1.1 is Scala 2.9.2 but the Kafka source code can also be compiled from other Scala versions as well, such as 2.8.0, 2.8.2, 2.9.1, or 2.10.1. Use the following the command to build the Kafka source:

```
[root@localhost opt]# ./gradlew -PscalaVersion=2.9.1 jar
```

In Kafka 8.x onwards, the Gradle tool is used to compile the Kafka source code (available in `kafka-0.8.1.1-src.tgz`) and build the Kafka binaries (JAR files). Similar to Kafka JAR, the unit test or source JAR can also be built using the Gradle build tool. For more information on build-related instructions, refer to `https://github.com/apache/kafka/blob/0.8.1/README.md`.

Summary

In this chapter, we have seen how companies are evolving the mechanism of collecting and processing application-generated data, and are learning to utilize the real power of this data by running analytics over it.

You also learned how to install 0.8.1.x. The following chapter discusses the steps required to set up single- or multi-broker Kafka clusters.

2
Setting Up a Kafka Cluster

Now we are ready to play with the Apache Kafka publisher-subscriber messaging system. With Kafka, we can create multiple types of clusters, such as the following:

- A single node—single broker cluster
- A single node—multiple broker clusters
- Multiple nodes—multiple broker clusters

A Kafka cluster primarily has five main components:

- **Topic**: A topic is a category or feed name to which messages are published by the message producers. In Kafka, topics are partitioned and each partition is represented by the ordered immutable sequence of messages. A Kafka cluster maintains the partitioned log for each topic. Each message in the partition is assigned a unique sequential ID called the *offset*.

- **Broker**: A Kafka cluster consists of one or more servers where each one may have one or more server processes running and is called the broker. Topics are created within the context of broker processes.

- **Zookeeper**: ZooKeeper serves as the coordination interface between the Kafka broker and consumers. The ZooKeeper overview given on the Hadoop Wiki site is as follows (`http://wiki.apache.org/hadoop/ZooKeeper/ProjectDescription`):

  > "*ZooKeeper allows distributed processes to coordinate with each other through a shared hierarchical name space of data registers (we call these registers znodes), much like a file system.*"

  The main differences between ZooKeeper and standard filesystems are that every znode can have data associated with it and znodes are limited to the amount of data that they can have. ZooKeeper was designed to store coordination data: status information, configuration, location information, and so on.

- **Producers**: Producers publish data to the topics by choosing the appropriate partition within the topic. For load balancing, the allocation of messages to the topic partition can be done in a round-robin fashion or using a custom defined function.

- **Consumer**: Consumers are the applications or processes that subscribe to topics and process the feed of published messages.

So let's start with a very basic cluster setup.

A single node – a single broker cluster

This is the starting point for learning Kafka. In the previous chapter, we installed Kafka on a single machine. Now it is time to set up a single node - single broker-based Kafka cluster, as shown in the following diagram:

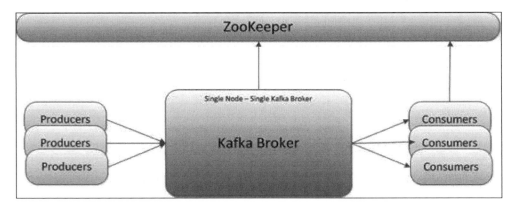

Starting the ZooKeeper server

Kafka provides the default and simple ZooKeeper configuration file used to launch a single local ZooKeeper instance although separate ZooKeeper installation can also be carried out while setting up the Kafka cluster. First start the local ZooKeeper instance using the following command:

```
[root@localhost kafka_2.9.2-0.8.1.1]# bin/zookeeper-server-start.sh
config/zookeeper.properties
```

You should get output as shown in the following screenshot:

```
[2014-08-27 03:55:25,705] INFO Server environment:user.name=root (org.apache.z
ookeeper.server.ZooKeeperServer)
[2014-08-27 03:55:25,705] INFO Server environment:user.home=/root (org.apache.
zookeeper.server.ZooKeeperServer)
[2014-08-27 03:55:25,706] INFO Server environment:user.dir=/opt/kafka_2.9.2-0.
8.1.1 (org.apache.zookeeper.server.ZooKeeperServer)
[2014-08-27 03:55:25,769] INFO tickTime set to 3000 (org.apache.zookeeper.serv
er.ZooKeeperServer)
[2014-08-27 03:55:25,769] INFO minSessionTimeout set to -1 (org.apache.zookeep
er.server.ZooKeeperServer)
[2014-08-27 03:55:25,769] INFO maxSessionTimeout set to -1 (org.apache.zookeep
er.server.ZooKeeperServer)
[2014-08-27 03:55:25,930] INFO binding to port 0.0.0.0/0.0.0.0:2181 (org.apach
e.zookeeper.server.NIOServerCnxn)
[2014-08-27 03:55:26,012] INFO Snapshotting: 0 (org.apache.zookeeper.server.pe
rsistence.FileTxnSnapLog)
```

 Kafka comes with the required property files defining minimal properties required for a single broker—single node cluster.

The important properties defined in `zookeeper.properties` are shown in the following code:

```
# Data directory where the zookeeper snapshot is stored.
dataDir=/tmp/zookeeper

# The port listening for client request
clientPort=2181
# disable the per-ip limit on the number of connections since this is
a non-production config
maxClientCnxns=0
```

By default, the ZooKeeper server will listen on `*:2181/tcp`. For detailed information on how to set up multiple ZooKeeper servers, visit `http://zookeeper.apache.org/`.

Starting the Kafka broker

Now start the Kafka broker in the new console window using the following command:

```
[root@localhost kafka_2.9.2-0.8.1.1]# bin/kafka-server-start.sh config/
server.properties
```

You should now see output as shown in the following screenshot:

```
[2014-08-27 04:04:12,968] INFO Awaiting socket connections on 0.0.0.0:9092. (k
afka.network.Acceptor)
[2014-08-27 04:04:13,005] INFO [Socket Server on Broker 0], Started (kafka.net
work.SocketServer)
[2014-08-27 04:04:13,335] INFO Will not load MX4J, mx4j-tools.jar is not in th
e classpath (kafka.utils.Mx4jLoader$)
[2014-08-27 04:04:13,602] INFO 0 successfully elected as leader (kafka.server.
ZookeeperLeaderElector)
[2014-08-27 04:04:13,864] INFO Registered broker 0 at path /brokers/ids/0 with
 address localhost:9092. (kafka.utils.ZkUtils$)
[2014-08-27 04:04:13,898] INFO [Kafka Server 0], started (kafka.server.KafkaSe
rver)
[2014-08-27 04:04:14,143] INFO New leader is 0 (kafka.server.ZookeeperLeaderEl
ector$LeaderChangeListener)
```

The `server.properties` file defines the following important properties required for the Kafka broker:

```
# The id of the broker. This must be set to a unique integer for each
broker.
Broker.id=0

# The port the socket server listens on
port=9092

# The directory under which to store log files
log.dir=/tmp/kafka8-logs

# The default number of log partitions per topic.
num.partitions=2

# Zookeeper connection string
zookeeper.connect=localhost:2181
```

The last section in this chapter defines a few additional and important properties available for the Kafka broker.

Creating a Kafka topic

Kafka provides a command line utility to create topics on the Kafka server. Let's create a topic named `kafkatopic` with a single partition and only one replica using this utility:

```
[root@localhost kafka_2.9.2-0.8.1.1]#bin/kafka-topics.sh --create
--zookeeper localhost:2181 --replication-factor 1 --partitions 1 --topic
kafkatopic


Created topic "kafkatopic".
```

You should get output on the Kafka server window as shown in the following screenshot:

```
ector$LeaderChangeListener)
[2014-08-27 04:16:26,943] INFO [ReplicaFetcherManager on broker 0] Removed fet
cher for partitions [kafkatopic,0] (kafka.server.ReplicaFetcherManager)
[2014-08-27 04:16:27,106] INFO Completed load of log kafkatopic-0 with log end
 offset 0 (kafka.log.Log)
[2014-08-27 04:16:27,118] INFO Created log for partition [kafkatopic,0] in /tm
p/kafka-logs with properties {segment.index.bytes -> 10485760, file.delete.del
ay.ms -> 60000, segment.bytes -> 536870912, flush.ms -> 9223372036854775807, d
elete.retention.ms -> 86400000, index.interval.bytes -> 4096, retention.bytes
-> -1, cleanup.policy -> delete, segment.ms -> 604800000, max.message.bytes ->
 1000012, flush.messages -> 9223372036854775807, min.cleanable.dirty.ratio ->
0.5, retention.ms -> 604800000}. (kafka.log.LogManager)
[2014-08-27 04:16:27,120] WARN Partition [kafkatopic,0] on broker 0: No checkp
ointed highwatermark is found for partition [kafkatopic,0] (kafka.cluster.Part
ition)
```

The `kafka-topics.sh` utility will create a topic, override the default number of partitions from two to one, and show a successful creation message. It also takes ZooKeeper server information, as in this case: `localhost:2181`. To get a list of topics on any Kafka server, use the following command in a new console window:

```
[root@localhost kafka_2.9.2-0.8.1.1]# bin/kafka-topics.sh --list
--zookeeper localhost:2181

kafkatopic
```

Starting a producer to send messages

Kafka provides users with a command line producer client that accepts inputs from the command line and publishes them as a message to the Kafka cluster. By default, each new line entered is considered as a new message. The following command is used to start the console-based producer in a new console window to send the messages:

```
[root@localhost kafka_2.9.2-0.8.1.1]# bin/kafka-console-producer.sh
--broker-list localhost:9092 --topic kafkatopic
```

The output will be as shown in the following screenshot:

```
[root@localhost kafka_2.9.2-0.8.1.1]# bin/kafka-console-producer.sh --broker-l
ist localhost:9092 --topic kafkatopic
SLF4J: Class path contains multiple SLF4J bindings.
SLF4J: Found binding in [jar:file:/opt/kafka_2.9.2-0.8.1.1/libs/slf4j-jdk14-1.
7.7.jar!/org/slf4j/impl/StaticLoggerBinder.class]
SLF4J: Found binding in [jar:file:/opt/kafka_2.9.2-0.8.1.1/libs/slf4j-log4j12-
1.7.7.jar!/org/slf4j/impl/StaticLoggerBinder.class]
SLF4J: Found binding in [jar:file:/opt/kafka_2.9.2-0.8.1.1/libs/slf4j-nop-1.7.
7.jar!/org/slf4j/impl/StaticLoggerBinder.class]
SLF4J: Found binding in [jar:file:/opt/kafka_2.9.2-0.8.1.1/libs/slf4j-simple-1
.7.7.jar!/org/slf4j/impl/StaticLoggerBinder.class]
SLF4J: See http://www.slf4j.org/codes.html#multiple_bindings for an explanatio
n.
SLF4J: Actual binding is of type [org.slf4j.impl.JDK14LoggerFactory]
```

While starting the producer's command line client, the following parameters are required:

- `broker-list`
- `topic`

The `broker-list` parameter specifies the brokers to be connected as `<node_address:port>`—that is, `localhost:9092`. The `kafkatopic` topic was created in the *Creating a Kafka topic* section. The topic name is required to send a message to a specific group of consumers who have subscribed to the same topic, `kafkatopic`.

Now type the following messages on the console window:

- Type `Welcome to Kafka` and press *Enter*
- Type `This is single broker cluster` and press *Enter*

You should see output as shown in the following screenshot:

```
SLF4J: Actual binding is of type [org.slf4j.impl.JDK14LoggerFactory]

Welcome to Kafka
This is single broker cluster
```

Try some more messages. The default properties for the consumer are defined in `producer.properties`. The important properties are:

```
# list of brokers used for bootstrapping knowledge about the rest of
the cluster
# format: host1:port1,host2:port2 ...
metadata.broker.list=localhost:9092
```

```
# specify the compression codec for all data generated: none , gzip,
snappy.
compression.codec=none
```

Detailed information about how to write producers for Kafka and producer properties will be discussed in *Chapter 4, Writing Producers.*

Starting a consumer to consume messages

Kafka also provides a command line consumer client for message consumption. The following command is used to start a console-based consumer that shows the output at the command line as soon as it subscribes to the topic created in the Kafka broker:

```
[root@localhost kafka_2.9.2-0.8.1.1]# bin/kafka-console-consumer.sh
--zookeeper localhost:2181 --topic kafkatopic --from-beginning
```

On execution of the previous command, you should get output as shown in the following screenshot:

```
SLF4J: Found binding in [jar:file:/opt/kafka_2.9.2-0.8.1.1/libs/slf4j-log4j12-
1.7.7.jar!/org/slf4j/impl/StaticLoggerBinder.class]
SLF4J: Found binding in [jar:file:/opt/kafka_2.9.2-0.8.1.1/libs/slf4j-nop-1.7.
7.jar!/org/slf4j/impl/StaticLoggerBinder.class]
SLF4J: Found binding in [jar:file:/opt/kafka_2.9.2-0.8.1.1/libs/slf4j-simple-1
.7.7.jar!/org/slf4j/impl/StaticLoggerBinder.class]
SLF4J: See http://www.slf4j.org/codes.html#multiple_bindings for an explanatio
n.
SLF4J: Actual binding is of type [org.slf4j.impl.JDK14LoggerFactory]



Welcome to Kafka
This is single broker cluster
```

The default properties for the consumer are defined in `/config/consumer.properties`. The important properties are:

```
# consumer group id (A string that uniquely identifies a set of
consumers # within the same consumer group)
group.id=test-consumer-group
```

Detailed information about how to write consumers for Kafka and consumer properties is discussed in *Chapter 5, Writing Consumers.*

By running all four components (`zookeeper`, `broker`, `producer`, and `consumer`) in different terminals, you will be able to enter messages from the producer's terminal and see them appearing in the subscribed consumer's terminal.

Usage information for both producer and consumer command line tools can be viewed by running the command with no arguments.

A single node – multiple broker clusters

Now we have come to the next level of the Kafka cluster. Let us now set up a single node - multiple broker-based Kafka cluster as shown in the following diagram:

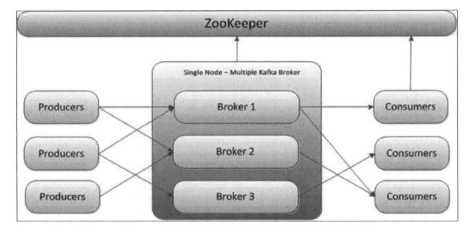

Starting ZooKeeper

The first step in starting ZooKeeper remains the same for this type of cluster.

Starting the Kafka broker

For setting up multiple brokers on a single node, different server property files are required for each broker. Each property file will define unique, different values for the following properties:

- `broker.id`
- `port`
- `log.dir`

For example, in `server-1.properties` used for `broker1`, we define the following:

- `broker.id=1`
- `port=9093`
- `log.dir=/tmp/kafka-logs-1`

Similarly, for `server-2.properties`, which is used for `broker2`, we define the following:

- `broker.id=2`
- `port=9094`
- `log.dir=/tmp/kafka-logs-2`

A similar procedure is followed for all new brokers. While defining the properties, we have changed the port numbers as all additional brokers will still be running on the same machine but, in the production environment, brokers will run on multiple machines. Now we start each new broker in a separate console window using the following commands:

```
[root@localhost kafka_2.9.2-0.8.1.1]# bin/kafka-server-start.sh config/
server-1.properties
```

```
[root@localhost kafka_2.9.2-0.8.1.1]# bin/kafka-server-start.sh config/
server-2.properties
```

...

Creating a Kafka topic using the command line

Using the command line utility for creating topics on the Kafka server, let's create a topic named `replicated-kafkatopic` with two partitions and two replicas:

```
[root@localhost kafka_2.9.2-0.8.1.1]# bin/kafka-topics.sh --create
--zookeeper localhost:2181 --replication-factor 3 --partitions 1 --topic
replicated-kafkatopic
```

```
Created topic "replicated-kafkatopic".
```

Starting a producer to send messages

If we use a single producer to get connected to all the brokers, we need to pass the initial list of brokers, and the information of the remaining brokers is identified by querying the broker passed within `broker-list`, as shown in the following command. This metadata information is based on the topic name:

```
--broker-list localhost:9092, localhost:9093
```

Use the following command to start the producer:

```
[root@localhost kafka_2.9.2-0.8.1.1]# bin/kafka-console-producer.
sh --broker-list localhost:9092, localhost:9093 --topic replicated-
kafkatopic
```

If we have a requirement to run multiple producers connecting to different combinations of brokers, we need to specify the broker list for each producer as we did in the case of multiple brokers.

Starting a consumer to consume messages

The same consumer client, as in the previous example, will be used in this process. Just as before, it shows the output on the command line as soon as it subscribes to the topic created in the Kafka broker:

```
[root@localhost kafka_2.9.2-0.8.1.1]# bin/kafka-console-consumer.sh
--zookeeper localhost:2181 --from-beginning --topic replicated-kafkatopic
```

Multiple nodes – multiple broker clusters

This cluster scenario is not discussed in detail in this book but, as in the case of the single node—multiple broker Kafka cluster, where we set up multiple brokers on each node, we should install Kafka on each node of the cluster, and all the brokers from the different nodes need to connect to the same ZooKeeper.

For testing purposes, all the commands will remain identical to the ones we used in the single node—multiple brokers cluster.

The following diagram shows the cluster scenario where multiple brokers are configured on multiple nodes (Node 1 and Node 2, in this case), and the producers and consumers are connected in different combinations:

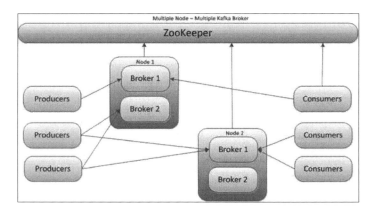

The Kafka broker property list

The following is the list of a few important properties that can be configured for the Kafka broker. For the complete list, visit `http://kafka.apache.org/documentation.html#brokerconfig`.

Property name	Description	Default value
`broker.id`	Each broker is uniquely identified by a non-negative integer ID. This ID serves as the broker's name and allows the broker to be moved to a different host/port without confusing consumers.	0
`log.dirs`	These are the directories in which the log data is stored. Each new partition that is created will be placed in the directory that currently has the fewest partitions.	`/tmp/kafka-logs`
`zookeeper.connect`	This specifies the ZooKeeper's connection string in the `hostname:port/chroot` form. Here, `chroot` is a base directory that is prepended to all path operations (this effectively namespaces all Kafka znodes to allow sharing with other applications on the same ZooKeeper cluster).	`localhost:2181`
`host.name`	This is the hostname of the broker. If this is set, it will only bind to this address. If this is not set, it will bind to all interfaces, and publish one to ZooKeeper.	`Null`
`num.partitions`	This is the default number of partitions per topic if a partition count isn't given at the time of topic creation.	1
`auto.create.topics.enable`	This enables auto-creation of the topic on the server. If this is set to true, then attempts to produce, consume, or fetch metadata for a non-existent topic will automatically create it with the default replication factor and number of partitions.	`True`
`default.replication.factor`	This is the default replication factor for automatically created topics.	1

Summary

In this chapter, you learned how to set up a Kafka cluster with single/multiple brokers on a single node, run command line producers and consumers, and exchange some messages. We also discussed important settings for the Kafka broker.

In the next chapter, we will look at the internal design of Kafka.

3
Kafka Design

Before we start getting our hands dirty by coding Kafka producers and consumers, let's quickly discuss the internal design of Kafka.

In this chapter, we shall be focusing on the following topics:

- Kafka design fundamentals
- Message compression in Kafka
- Replication in Kafka

Due to the overheads associated with JMS and its various implementations and limitations with the scaling architecture, LinkedIn (`www.linkedin.com`) decided to build Kafka to address its need for monitoring activity stream data and operational metrics such as CPU, I/O usage, and request timings.

While developing Kafka, the main focus was to provide the following:

- An API for producers and consumers to support custom implementation
- Low overheads for network and storage with message persistence on disk
- A high throughput supporting millions of messages for both publishing and subscribing—for example, real-time log aggregation or data feeds
- Distributed and highly scalable architecture to handle low-latency delivery
- Auto-balancing multiple consumers in the case of failure
- Guaranteed fault-tolerance in the case of server failures

Kafka design fundamentals

Kafka is neither a queuing platform where messages are received by a single consumer out of the consumer pool, nor a publisher-subscriber platform where messages are published to all the consumers. In a very basic structure, a producer publishes messages to a Kafka topic (synonymous with "messaging queue"). A topic is also considered as a message category or feed name to which messages are published. Kafka topics are created on a Kafka broker acting as a Kafka server. Kafka brokers also store the messages if required. Consumers then subscribe to the Kafka topic (one or more) to get the messages. Here, brokers and consumers use Zookeeper to get the state information and to track message offsets, respectively. This is described in the following diagram:

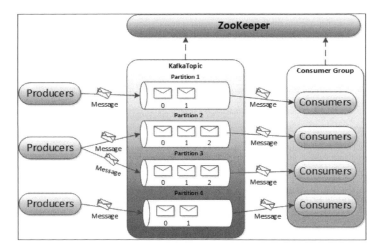

In the preceding diagram, a single node—single broker architecture is shown with a topic having four partitions. In terms of the components, the preceding diagram shows all the five components of the Kafka cluster: Zookeeper, Broker, Topic, Producer, and Consumer.

In Kafka topics, every partition is mapped to a logical log file that is represented as a set of segment files of equal sizes. Every partition is an ordered, immutable sequence of messages; each time a message is published to a partition, the broker appends the message to the last segment file. These segment files are flushed to disk after configurable numbers of messages have been published or after a certain amount of time has elapsed. Once the segment file is flushed, messages are made available to the consumers for consumption.

All the message partitions are assigned a unique sequential number called the *offset*, which is used to identify each message within the partition. Each partition is optionally replicated across a configurable number of servers for fault tolerance.

Each partition available on either of the servers acts as the *leader* and has zero or more servers acting as *followers*. Here the leader is responsible for handling all read and write requests for the partition while the followers asynchronously replicate data from the leader. Kafka dynamically maintains a set of **in-sync replicas (ISR)** that are caught-up to the leader and always persist the latest ISR set to ZooKeeper. In if the leader fails, one of the followers (in-sync replicas) will automatically become the new leader. In a Kafka cluster, each server plays a dual role; it acts as a leader for some of its partitions and also a follower for other partitions. This ensures the load balance within the Kafka cluster.

The Kafka platform is built based on what has been learned from both the traditional platforms and has the concept of consumer groups. Here, each consumer is represented as a process and these processes are organized within groups called **consumer groups**.

A message within a topic is consumed by a single process (consumer) within the consumer group and, if the requirement is such that a single message is to be consumed by multiple consumers, all these consumers need to be kept in different consumer groups. Consumers always consume messages from a particular partition sequentially and also acknowledge the message offset. This acknowledgement implies that the consumer has consumed all prior messages. Consumers issue an asynchronous pull request containing the offset of the message to be consumed to the broker and get the buffer of bytes.

In line with Kafka's design, brokers are stateless, which means the message state of any consumed message is maintained within the message consumer, and the Kafka broker does not maintain a record of what is consumed by whom. If this is poorly implemented, the consumer ends up in reading the same message multiple times. If the message is deleted from the broker (as the broker doesn't know whether the message is consumed or not), Kafka defines the time-based SLA (service level agreement) as a message retention policy. In line with this policy, a message will be automatically deleted if it has been retained in the broker longer than the defined SLA period. This message retention policy empowers consumers to deliberately rewind to an old offset and re-consume data although, as with traditional messaging systems, this is a violation of the queuing contract with consumers.

Let's discuss the message delivery semantic Kafka provides between producer and consumer. There are multiple possible ways to deliver messages, such as:

- Messages are never redelivered but may be lost
- Messages may be redelivered but never lost
- Messages are delivered once and only once

When publishing, a message is committed to the log. If a producer experiences a network error while publishing, it can never be sure if this error happened before or after the message was committed. Once committed, the message will not be lost as long as either of the brokers that replicate the partition to which this message was written remains available. For guaranteed message publishing, configurations such as getting acknowledgements and the waiting time for messages being committed are provided at the producer's end.

From the consumer point-of-view, replicas have exactly the same log with the same offsets, and the consumer controls its position in this log. For consumers, Kafka guarantees that the message will be delivered at least once by reading the messages, processing the messages, and finally saving their position. If the consumer process crashes after processing messages but before saving their position, another consumer process takes over the topic partition and may receive the first few messages, which are already processed.

Log compaction

Log compaction is a mechanism to achieve finer-grained, per-message retention, rather than coarser-grained, time-based retention. It ensures that the last known value for each message key within the log for a topic partition must be retained by removing the records where a more recent update with the same primary key is done. Log compaction also addresses system failure cases or system restarts, and so on.

In the Kafka cluster, the retention policy can be set on a per-topic basis such as time based, size-based, or log compaction-based. Log compaction ensures the following:

- Ordering of messages is always maintained
- The messages will have sequential offsets and the offset never changes
- Reads progressing from offset 0, or the consumer progressing from the start of the log, will see at least the final state of all records in the order they were written

Log compaction is handled by a pool of background threads that recopy log segment files, removing records whose key appears in the head of the log.

The following points summarize important Kafka design facts:

- The fundamental backbone of Kafka is message caching and storing on the fiesystem. In Kafka, data is immediately written to the OS kernel page. Caching and flushing of data to the disk are configurable.
- Kafka provides longer retention of messages even after consumption, allowing consumers to re-consume, if required.

- Kafka uses a message set to group messages to allow lesser network overhead.

- Unlike most messaging systems, where metadata of the consumed messages are kept at the server level, in Kafka the state of the consumed messages is maintained at the consumer level. This also addresses issues such as:

  ○ Losing messages due to failure

  ○ Multiple deliveries of the same message

  By default, consumers store the state in Zookeeper but Kafka also allows storing it within other storage systems used for **Online Transaction Processing (OLTP)** applications as well.

- In Kafka, producers and consumers work on the traditional push-and-pull model, where producers push the message to a Kafka broker and consumers pull the message from the broker.

- Kafka does not have any concept of a master and treats all the brokers as peers. This approach facilitates addition and removal of a Kafka broker at any point, as the metadata of brokers are maintained in Zookeeper and shared with consumers.

- Producers also have an option to choose between asynchronous or synchronous mode to send messages to a broker.

Message compression in Kafka

For the cases where network bandwidth is a bottleneck, Kafka provides a message group compression feature for efficient message delivery. Kafka supports efficient compression by allowing recursive message sets where the compressed message may have infinite depth relative to messages within itself. Efficient compression requires compressing multiple messages together rather than compressing each message individually. A batch of messages is compressed together and sent to the broker. There is a reduced network overhead for the compressed message set and decompression also attracts very little additional overhead.

In an earlier version of Kafka, 0.7, compressed batches of messages remained compressed in the log files and were presented as a single message to the consumer who later decompressed it. Hence, the additional overhead of decompression was present only at the consumer's end.

In Kafka 0.8, changes were made to the broker in the way it handles message offsets; this may also cause a degradation in broker performance in the case of compressed messages.

In Kafka 0.7, messages were addressable by physical byte offsets in the partition's log whereas in Kafka 0.8 each message is addressable by a non-comparable, increasingly logical offset that is unique per partition—that is, the first message has an offset of 1, the tenth message has an offset of 10, and so on. In Kafka 0.8, changes to offset management simplify the consumer capability to rewind the message offset.

In Kafka 0.8, the lead broker is responsible for serving the messages for a partition by assigning unique logical offsets to every message before it is appended to the logs. In the case of compressed data, the lead broker has to decompress the message set in order to assign offsets to the messages inside the compressed message set. Once offsets are assigned, the leader again compresses the data and then appends it to the disk. The lead broker follows this process for every compressed message sets it receives, which causes CPU load on a Kafka broker.

In Kafka, data is compressed by the message producer using either the **GZIP** or **Snappy** compression protocols. The following producer configurations need to be provided to use compression at the producer's end.

Property name	Description	Default value
compression. codec	This parameter specifies the compression codec for all data generated by this producer. Valid values are none, gzip, and snappy.	none
compressed. topics	This parameter allows you to set whether compression should be turned on for particular topics. If the compression codec is anything other than none, enable compression only for specified topics, if any. If the list of compressed topics is empty, then enable the specified compression codec for all topics. If the compression codec is none, compression is disabled for all topics.	null

The ByteBufferMessageSet class representing message sets may consist of both uncompressed as well as compressed data. To differentiate between compressed and uncompressed messages, a compression-attributes byte is introduced in the message header. Within this compression byte, the lowest two bits are used to represent the compression codec used for compression and the value 0 of these last two bits represents an uncompressed message.

Message compression techniques are very useful for mirroring data across datacenters using Kafka, where large amounts of data get transferred from active to passive datacenters in the compressed format.

Replication in Kafka

Before we talk about replication in Kafka, let's talk about message partitioning. In Kafka, a message partitioning strategy is used at the Kafka broker end. The decision about how the message is partitioned is taken by the producer, and the broker stores the messages in the same order as they arrive. The number of partitions can be configured for each topic within the Kafka broker.

Kafka replication is one of the very important features introduced in Kafka 0.8. Though Kafka is highly scalable, for better durability of messages and high availability of Kafka clusters, replication guarantees that the message will be published and consumed even in the case of broker failure, which may be caused by any reason. Both producers and consumers are replication-aware in Kafka. The following diagram explains replication in Kafka:

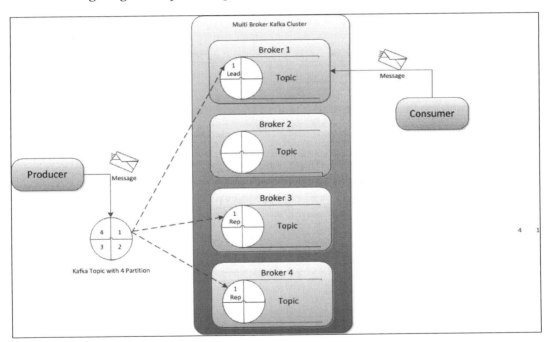

Let's discuss the preceding diagram in detail.

In replication, each partition of a message has *n* replicas and can afford *n-1* failures to guarantee message delivery. Out of the *n* replicas, one replica acts as the lead replica for the rest of the replicas. Zookeeper keeps the information about the lead replica and the current follower **in-sync replicas** (**ISR**). The lead replica maintains the list of all in-sync follower replicas.

Each replica stores its part of the message in local logs and offsets, and is periodically synced to the disk. This process also ensures that either a message is written to all the replicas or to none of them.

Kafka supports the following replication modes:

- **Synchronous replication**: In synchronous replication, a producer first identifies the lead replica from ZooKeeper and publishes the message. As soon as the message is published, it is written to the log of the lead replica and all the followers of the lead start pulling the message; by using a single channel, the order of messages is ensured. Each follower replica sends an acknowledgement to the lead replica once the message is written to its respective logs. Once replications are complete and all expected acknowledgements are received, the lead replica sends an acknowledgement to the producer. On the consumer's side, all the pulling of messages is done from the lead replica.

- **Asynchronous replication**: The only difference in this mode is that, as soon as a lead replica writes the message to its local log, it sends the acknowledgement to the message client and does not wait for acknowledgements from follower replicas. But, as a downside, this mode does not ensure message delivery in case of a broker failure.

If any of the follower in-sync replicas fail, the leader drops the failed follower from its ISR list after the configured timeout period and writes will continue on the remaining replicas in ISRs. Whenever the failed follower comes back, it first truncates its log to the last checkpoint (the offset of the last committed message) and then starts to catch up with all messages from the leader, starting from the checkpoint. As soon as the follower becomes fully synced with the leader, the leader adds it back to the current ISR list.

If the lead replica fails, either while writing the message partition to its local log or before sending the acknowledgement to the message producer, a message partition is resent by the producer to the new lead broker.

The process of choosing the new lead replica involves all the followers' ISRs registering themselves with Zookeeper. The very first registered replica becomes the new lead replica and its **log end offset (LEO)** becomes the offset of the last committed message (also known as **high watermark (HW)**). The rest of the registered replicas become the followers of the newly elected leader. Each replica registers a listener in Zookeeper so that it will be informed of any leader change. Whenever the new leader is elected and the notified replica is not the leader, it truncates its log to the offset of the last committed message and then starts to catch up from the new leader. The new elected leader waits either until the time configured is passed or until all live replicas get in sync and then the leader writes the current ISR to Zookeeper and opens itself up for both message reads and writes.

Replication in Kafka ensures stronger durability and higher availability. It guarantees that any successfully published message will not be lost and will be consumed, even in the case of broker failures.

 For more insight on Kafka replication implementation, visit `https://cwiki.apache.org/confluence/display/KAFKA/kafka+Detailed+Replication+Design+V3`.

Summary

In this chapter, you learned the design concepts used to build a solid foundation for Kafka. You also learned how message compression and replication are done in Kafka.

In the next chapter, we will be focusing on how to write Kafka producers using the API provided.

4

Writing Producers

Producers are applications that create messages and publish them to the Kafka broker for further consumption. These producers can be different in nature; for example, frontend applications, backend services, proxy applications, adapters to legacy systems, and producers for Hadoop. These producers can also be implemented in different languages such as Java, C, and Python.

In this chapter, we will be focusing on the following topics:

- The Kafka API for message producers
- Java-based Kafka producers
- Java-based producers using custom message partitioning

At the end of the chapter, we will also explore a few important configurations required for the Kafka producer.

Let's begin. The following diagram explains the high-level working of Kafka producers in producing the messages:

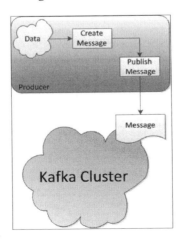

The producer connects to any of the alive nodes and requests metadata about the leaders for the partitions of a topic. This allows the producer to put the message directly to the lead broker for the partition.

The Kafka producer API exposes the interface for semantic partitioning by allowing the producer to specify a key to partition by and using this to hash to a partition. Thus, the producer can completely control which partition it publishes messages to; for example, if customer ID is selected as a key, then all data for a given customer will be sent to the same partition. This also allows data consumers to make locality assumptions about customer data.

For high efficiency in Kafka, producers can also publish the messages in batches that work in asynchronous mode only. In asynchronous mode, the producer works either with a fixed number of messages or fixed latency defined by producer configuration, `queue.time` or `batch.size`, respectively for example, 10 seconds or 50 messages. Data is accumulated in memory at the producer's end and published in batches in a single request. Asynchronous mode also brings the risk of losing the data in the case of a producer crash with accumulated non-published, in-memory data.

 For asynchronous producers, callback method functionality is proposed for future release; this would be used for registering handlers to catch sent errors.

In the next few sections, we will discuss the API provided by Kafka for writing Java-based custom producers.

The Java producer API

Let us first understand the important classes that are imported to write Java-based basic producers for a Kafka cluster:

- `Producer`: Kafka provides the `kafka.javaapi.producer.Producer` class (class `Producer<K, V>`) for creating messages for single or multiple topics with message partition as an optional feature. The default message partitioner is based on the hash of the key. Here, `Producer` is a type of Java generic (http://en.wikipedia.org/wiki/Generics_in_Java) written in Scala where we need to specify the type of parameters; `K` and `V` specify the types for the partition key and message value, respectively. The following is the class diagram and its explanation:

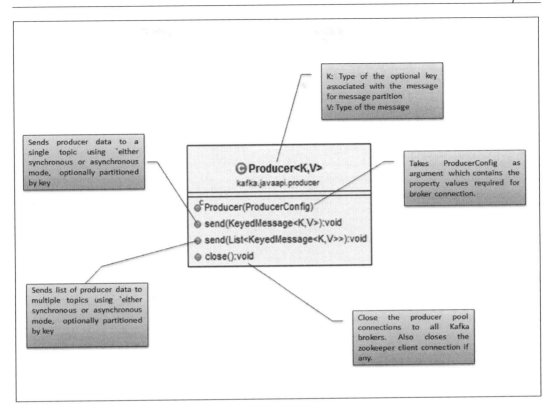

- KeyedMessage: The `kafka.producer.KeyedMessage` class takes the topic name, partition key, and the message value that need to be passed from the producer as follows:

```
class KeyedMessage[K, V](val topic: String, val key: K, val
message: V)
```

Here, `KeyedMessage` is a type of Java generic written in Scala where we need to specify the type of the parameters; `K` and `V` specify the type for the partition key and message value, respectively, and the topic is always of type `String`.

- ProducerConfig: The `kafka.producer.ProducerConfig` class encapsulates the values required for establishing the connection with the brokers such as the broker list, message partition class, serializer class for the message, and partition key.

The Producer API wraps the low-level producer implementations for synchronous (default behavior) and asynchronous producers that are picked up based on the producer configuration `producer.type`. For example, in the case of asynchronous producers the `kafka.producer.Producer` class handles the buffering of the producer's data before the data is serialized and dispatched to the appropriate Kafka broker partition. Internally, the `kafka.producer.async.ProducerSendThread` instance dequeues the batch of messages and `kafka.producer.EventHandler` serializes and dispatches the data. The Kafka producer configuration `event.handler` also provides the ability to define custom event handlers.

 All the examples are developed and tested for a multi-broker cluster (either single or multiple nodes). For more information on how to set up a single node - multi-broker cluster, refer to *Chapter 2, Setting Up a Kafka Cluster*.

Simple Java producers

Now we will start writing a simple Java-based producer to transmit the message to the broker. This `SimpleProducer` class is used to create a message for a specific topic and transmit it using the default message partitioning.

Importing classes

As the first step, we need to import the following classes:

```
import kafka.javaapi.producer.Producer;
import kafka.producer.KeyedMessage;
import kafka.producer.ProducerConfig;
```

Defining properties

As the next step in writing the producer, we need to define properties for making a connection with the Kafka broker and pass these properties to the Kafka producer:

```
Properties props = new Properties();
props.put("metadata.broker.list","localhost:9092, localhost:9093,
localhost:9094");
props.put("serializer.class","kafka.serializer.StringEncoder");
props.put("request.required.acks", "1");
ProducerConfig config = new ProducerConfig(props);
Producer<String, String> producer = new Producer<String, String>
(config);
```

Now let us see the major properties mentioned in the code:

- `metadata.broker.list`: This property specifies the list of brokers (in the [<node:port>, <node:port>] format) that the producer needs to connect to. Kafka producers automatically determine the lead broker for the topic, partition it by raising a request for the metadata, and connect to the correct broker before it publishes any message.

- `serializer.class`: This property specifies the `serializer` class that needs to be used while preparing the message for transmission from the producer to the broker. In this example, we will be using the string encoder provided by Kafka. By default, the `serializer` class for the key and message is the same, but we can also implement the custom `serializer` class by extending the Scala-based `kafka.serializer.Encoder` implementation. Producer configuration `key.serializer.class` is used to set the custom encoder.

- `request.required.acks`: This property instructs the Kafka broker to send an acknowledgment to the producer when a message is received. The value `1` means the producer receives an acknowledgment once the lead replica has received the data. This option provides better durability as the producer waits until the broker acknowledges the request as successful. By default, the producer works in the "fire and forget" mode and is not informed in the case of message loss.

Building the message and sending it

As the final step, we need to build the message and send it to the broker as shown in the following code:

```
String runtime = new Date().toString();;
String msg = "Message Publishing Time - " + runtime;
KeyedMessage<String, String> data = new KeyedMessage<String, String>
(topic, msg);
producer.send(data);
```

The complete program will look as follows:

```
package kafka.examples.ch4;

import java.util.Date;
import java.util.Properties;

import kafka.javaapi.producer.Producer;
import kafka.producer.KeyedMessage;
import kafka.producer.ProducerConfig;
```

```
public class SimpleProducer {
  private static Producer<String, String> producer;

  public SimpleProducer() {
    Properties props = new Properties();

    // Set the broker list for requesting metadata to find the lead
broker
    props.put("metadata.broker.list",
           "192.168.146.132:9092, 192.168.146.132:9093,
192.168.146.132:9094");

    //This specifies the serializer class for keys
    props.put("serializer.class", "kafka.serializer.StringEncoder");

    // 1 means the producer receives an acknowledgment once the lead
replica
    // has received the data. This option provides better durability
as the
    // client waits until the server acknowledges the request as
successful.
    props.put("request.required.acks", "1");

    ProducerConfig config = new ProducerConfig(props);
    producer = new Producer<String, String>(config);
  }

  public static void main(String[] args) {
    int argsCount = args.length;
    if (argsCount == 0 || argsCount == 1)
      throw new IllegalArgumentException(
        "Please provide topic name and Message count as arguments");

    // Topic name and the message count to be published is passed from
the
    // command line
    String topic = (String) args[0];
    String count = (String) args[1];
    int messageCount = Integer.parseInt(count);
    System.out.println("Topic Name - " + topic);
    System.out.println("Message Count - " + messageCount);

    SimpleProducer simpleProducer = new SimpleProducer();
    simpleProducer.publishMessage(topic, messageCount);
  }

  private void publishMessage(String topic, int messageCount) {
```

```
for (int mCount = 0; mCount < messageCount; mCount++) {
  String runtime = new Date().toString();

  String msg = "Message Publishing Time - " + runtime;
  System.out.println(msg);
  // Creates a KeyedMessage instance
  KeyedMessage<String, String> data =
    new KeyedMessage<String, String>(topic, msg);

  // Publish the message
  producer.send(data);
}
// Close producer connection with broker.
producer.close();
}
}
```

Before running this, make sure you have created the topic kafkatopic either using the API or from the command line, as follows:

```
[root@localhost kafka_2.9.2-0.8.1.1]#bin/kafka-topics.sh --create
--zookeeper localhost:2181 --replication-factor 1 --partitions 3 --topic
kafkatopic
```

Before compiling and running the Java-based Kafka program in the console, make sure you download the slf4j-1.7.7.tar.gz file from http://www.slf4j.org/download.html and copy slf4j-log4j12-1.7.7.jar contained within slf4j-1.7.7.tar.gz to the /opt/kafka_2.9.2-0.8.1.1/libs directory. Add the KAFKA_LIB environment variable and also add all the libraries available in /opt/kafka_2.9.2-0.8.1.1/libs to the classpath using the following commands:

```
[root@localhost kafka_2.9.2-0.8.1.1]# export KAFKA_
LIB=/opt/kafka_2.9.2-0.8.1.1/libs
[root@localhost kafka_2.9.2-0.8.1.1]# export
CLASSPATH=.:$KAFKA_LIB/jopt-simple-3.2.jar:$KAFKA_
LIB/kafka_2.9.2-0.8.1.1.jar:$KAFKA_LIB/log4j-1.2.15.
jar:$KAFKA_LIB/metrics-core-2.2.0.jar:$KAFKA_LIB/
scala-library-2.9.2.jar:$KAFKA_LIB/slf4j-api-
1.7.2.jar:$KAFKA_LIB/slf4j-log4j12-1.7.7.jar:$KAFKA_
LIB/snappy-java-1.0.5.jar:$KAFKA_LIB/zkclient-
0.3.jar:$KAFKA_LIB/zookeeper-3.3.4.jar
```

Compile the preceding program using the following command:

```
[root@localhost kafka_2.9.2-0.8.1.1]# javac -d . kafka/examples/ch4/
SimpleProducer.java
```

Run the simple producer using the following command:

```
[root@localhost kafka_2.9.2-0.8.1.1]# java kafka.examples.ch4.
SimpleProducer kafkatopic 10
```

The `SimpleProducer` class takes two arguments; first, the topic name and second, the number of messages to be published. Once the producer is successfully executed and begins publishing the messages to the broker, run the command line consumer for consuming the messages as it subscribes to the topic created in the Kafka broker as:

```
[root@localhost kafka_2.9.2-0.8.1.1]# bin/kafka-console-consumer.sh
--zookeeper localhost:2181 --from-beginning --topic kafkatopic
```

Creating a Java producer with custom partitioning

The previous example is a very basic example of a `Producer` class running on a single-node, multi-broker cluster with no explicit partitioning of messages. Jumping to the next level, let's write another program that uses customized message partitioning. In this example, a log message for a website visit from any IP address is captured and published. This log message has three parts:

- The timestamp of the website hit
- The name of website itself
- The IP address from where the website is being accessed

Let's begin with the coding.

Importing classes

First import the following classes:

```
import java.util.Date;
import java.util.Properties;
import java.util.Random;

import kafka.javaapi.producer.Producer;
import kafka.producer.KeyedMessage;
import kafka.producer.ProducerConfig;
```

Defining properties

As the next step, we need to define properties for making a connection with the Kafka broker, as shown in the following code, and pass these properties to the Kafka producer:

```
Properties props = new Properties();
props.put("metadata.broker.list","localhost:9092, localhost:9093,
localhost:9094");
props.put("serializer.class","kafka.serializer.StringEncoder");
props.put("partitioner.class", "kafka.examples.ch4.
SimplePartitioner");
props.put("request.required.acks", "1");
ProducerConfig config = new ProducerConfig(props);
Producer<Integer, String> producer = new Producer<Integer,
String>(config);
```

The only change in the previous property list is the addition of the `partitioner.class` configuration.

The `partitioner.class` property defines the class to be used for determining the partition in the topic where the message needs to be sent. If the key is null, Kafka uses the hash value of the key.

Implementing the Partitioner class

Next, we need to develop a custom partitioner class `SimplePartitioner` by implementing the `Partitioner` class (an abstract class written in Scala) that takes the key, which in this example is the IP address. It then finds the last octet and does a modulo operation on the number of partitions defined within Kafka for the topic. The following is the code for the `SimplePartitioner` class:

```
package kafka.examples.ch4;

import kafka.producer.Partitioner;

public class SimplePartitioner implements Partitioner {

  public SimplePartitioner (VerifiableProperties props) {

  }

  /*
   * The method takes the key, which in this case is the IP address,
   * It finds the last octet and does a modulo operation on the number
```

```
 * of partitions defined within Kafka for the topic.
 *
 * @see kafka.producer.Partitioner#partition(java.lang.Object, int)
 */
public int partition(Object key, int a_numPartitions) {
  int partition = 0;
  String partitionKey = (String) key;
  int offset = partitionKey.lastIndexOf('.');
  if (offset > 0) {
    partition = Integer.parseInt(partitionKey.substring(offset + 1))
        % a_numPartitions;
  }
  return partition;
}
}
```

Building the message and sending it

As the final step, we need to build the message and send it to the broker. The following is the complete listing of the program:

```
package kafka.examples.ch4;

import java.util.Date;
import java.util.Properties;
import java.util.Random;

import kafka.javaapi.producer.Producer;
import kafka.producer.KeyedMessage;
import kafka.producer.ProducerConfig;

public class CustomPartitionProducer {
  private static Producer<String, String> producer;

  public CustomPartitionProducer() {
    Properties props = new Properties();

    // Set the broker list for requesting metadata to find the lead
broker
    props.put("metadata.broker.list",
        "192.168.146.132:9092, 192.168.146.132:9093,
192.168.146.132:9094");
```

```
    // This specifies the serializer class for keys
    props.put("serializer.class", "kafka.serializer.StringEncoder");

    // Defines the class to be used for determining the partition
    // in the topic where the message needs to be sent.
    props.put("partitioner.class", "kafka.examples.ch4.
SimplePartitioner");

    // 1 means the producer receives an acknowledgment once the lead
replica
    // has received the data. This option provides better durability
as the
    // client waits until the server acknowledges the request as
successful.
    props.put("request.required.acks", "1");

    ProducerConfig config = new ProducerConfig(props);
    producer = new Producer<String, String>(config);
  }

  public static void main(String[] args) {
    int argsCount = args.length;
    if (argsCount == 0 || argsCount == 1)
      throw new IllegalArgumentException(
        "Please provide topic name and Message count as arguments");

    // Topic name and the message count to be published is passed from
the
    // command line
    String topic = (String) args[0];
    String count = (String) args[1];
    int messageCount = Integer.parseInt(count);

    System.out.println("Topic Name - " + topic);
    System.out.println("Message Count - " + messageCount);

    CustomPartitionProducer simpleProducer = new
CustomPartitionProducer();
    simpleProducer.publishMessage(topic, messageCount);
  }

  private void publishMessage(String topic, int messageCount) {
    Random random = new Random();
    for (int mCount = 0; mCount < messageCount; mCount++) {
```

```
        String clientIP = "192.168.14." + random.nextInt(255);
        String accessTime = new Date().toString();

        String message = accessTime + ",kafka.apache.org," + clientIP;
          System.out.println(message);

          // Creates a KeyedMessage instance
          KeyedMessage<String, String> data =
            new KeyedMessage<String, String>(topic, clientIP, message);

          // Publish the message
          producer.send(data);
        }
        // Close producer connection with broker.
        producer.close();
      }
    }
```

Before running this, make sure you have created the topic website-hits from the command line:

```
[root@localhost kafka_2.9.2-0.8.1.1]# bin/kafka-topics.sh --create
--zookeeper localhost:2181 --replication-factor 3 --partitions 5 --topic
website-hits
```

Also, as specified in the beginning of the previous example, do the classpath settings if not already done. Now compile the partitioner class and the preceding producer program using the following command:

```
[root@localhost kafka_2.9.2-0.8.1.1]# javac -d . kafka/examples/ch4/
SimplePartitioner.java
```

```
[root@localhost kafka_2.9.2-0.8.1.1]# javac -d . kafka/examples/ch4/
CustomPartitionProducer.java
```

Run the custom partition producer using the following command:

```
[root@localhost kafka_2.9.2-0.8.1.1]# java kafka.examples.ch4.
CustomPartitionProducer website-hits 100
```

The `CustomPartitionProducer` program takes two arguments; first, the topic name and second, the number of log messages to be published. Once the producer is successfully executed and begins publishing the messages to the broker, run the command line consumer for consuming the messages as it subscribes to the topic created in the Kafka broker:

```
[root@localhost kafka_2.9.2-0.8.1.1]# bin/kafka-console-consumer.sh
--zookeeper localhost:2181 --from-beginning --topic kafkatopic
```

In the preceding example, the benefit of using custom partitioning logic is that all the log messages that are generated for the same client IP address will end up going to the same partition. Also, the same partition may have batch log messages for different IP addresses.

> The partitioning logic also needs to be known to the consumer so that the consumer can consume the messages published for the desired IPs. This part is covered in *Chapter 5, Writing Consumers*.

The Kafka producer property list

The following table shows a list of a few important properties that can be configured for Kafka producer. The Scala class `kafka.producer.ProducerConfig` provides implementation-level details for producer configurations. For the complete list, visit `http://kafka.apache.org/documentation.html#producerconfigs`.

Property name	Description	Default value
`metadata.broker.list`	The producer uses this property to get metadata (topics, partitions, and replicas). The socket connections for sending the actual data will be established based on the broker information returned in the metadata. The format is `host1:port1,host2:port2`.	
`serializer.class`	This specifies the `serializer` class for the messages. The default encoder accepts a byte and returns the same byte.	`kafka.serializer.DefaultEncoder`
`producer.type`	This property specifies how the messages will be sent: • async for asynchronous sending (used with message batching) • sync for synchronous sending	`sync`

Property name	Description	Default value
request. required.acks	This value controls when the producer request is considered complete and whether the producer receives an acknowledgment from the broker: • 0 means the producer will never wait for an acknowledgment from the broker. This is used for the lowest latency, but with the weakest durability. • 1 means the producer receives an acknowledgment once the lead replica has received the data. This option provides better durability as the client waits until the server acknowledges the request as successful. • -1 means the producer will receive an acknowledgment once all the in-sync replicas have received the data. This option provides the best durability.	0
key. serializer. class	This specifies the serializer class for keys.	${serializer. class}
partitioner. class	This is the partitioner class for partitioning messages among subtopics. The default partitioner is based on the hash value of the key.	kafka. producer. Default Partitioner
compression. codec	This parameter specifies the compression codec for all data generated by this producer. Valid values are none, gzip, and snappy.	none
batch.num. messages	This specifies the number of messages to be sent in one batch when using async mode. The producer will wait until this quantity of messages is ready to be sent or queue. buffer.max.ms is reached.	200

Summary

In this chapter we have learned how to write basic producers and some advanced Java producers that use message partitioning. We have also covered the details of properties for Kafka producers.

In the next chapter, we will learn how to write Java-based consumers for message consumption.

5
Writing Consumers

Consumers are the applications that consume the messages published by Kafka producers and process the data extracted from them. Like producers, consumers can also be different in nature, such as applications doing real-time or near real-time analysis, applications with NoSQL or data warehousing solutions, backend services, consumers for Hadoop, or other subscriber-based solutions. These consumers can also be implemented in different languages such as Java, C, and Python.

In this chapter, we will focus on the following topics:

- The Kafka Consumer API
- Java-based Kafka consumers
- Java-based Kafka consumers consuming partitioned messages

At the end of the chapter, we will explore some of the important properties that can be set for a Kafka consumer. So, let's start.

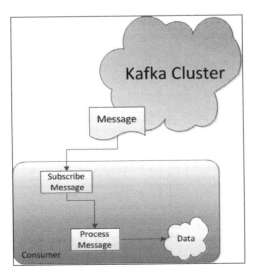

The preceding diagram explains the high-level working of the Kafka consumer when consuming the messages. The consumer subscribes to the message consumption from a specific topic on the Kafka broker. The consumer then issues a fetch request to the lead broker to consume the message partition by specifying the message offset (the beginning position of the message offset). Therefore, the Kafka consumer works in the pull model and always pulls all available messages after its current position in the Kafka log (the Kafka internal data representation).

While subscribing, the consumer connects to any of the live nodes and requests metadata about the leaders for the partitions of a topic. This allows the consumer to communicate directly with the lead broker receiving the messages. Kafka topics are divided into a set of ordered partitions and each partition is consumed by one consumer only. Once a partition is consumed, the consumer changes the message offset to the next partition to be consumed. This represents the states about what has been consumed and also provides the flexibility of deliberately rewinding back to an old offset and re-consuming the partition. In the next few sections, we will discuss the API provided by Kafka for writing Java-based custom consumers.

 All the Kafka classes referred to in this book are actually written in Scala.

Kafka consumer APIs

Kafka provides two types of API for Java consumers:

- High-level API
- Low-level API

The high-level consumer API

The high-level consumer API is used when only data is needed and the handling of message offsets is not required. This API hides broker details from the consumer and allows effortless communication with the Kafka cluster by providing an abstraction over the low-level implementation. The high-level consumer stores the last offset (the position within the message partition where the consumer left off consuming the message), read from a specific partition in Zookeeper. This offset is stored based on the consumer group name provided to Kafka at the beginning of the process.

The consumer group name is unique and global across the Kafka cluster and any new consumers with an in-use consumer group name may cause ambiguous behavior in the system. When a new process is started with the existing consumer group name, Kafka triggers a rebalance between the new and existing process threads for the consumer group. After the rebalance, some messages that are intended for a new process may go to an old process, causing unexpected results. To avoid this ambiguous behavior, any existing consumers should be shut down before starting new consumers for an existing consumer group name.

The following are the classes that are imported to write Java-based basic consumers using the high-level consumer API for a Kafka cluster:

- `ConsumerConnector`: Kafka provides the `ConsumerConnector` interface (`interface ConsumerConnector`) that is further implemented by the `ZookeeperConsumerConnector` class (`kafka.javaapi.consumer.ZookeeperConsumerConnector`). This class is responsible for all the interaction a consumer has with ZooKeeper.

  The following is the class diagram for the `ConsumerConnector` class:

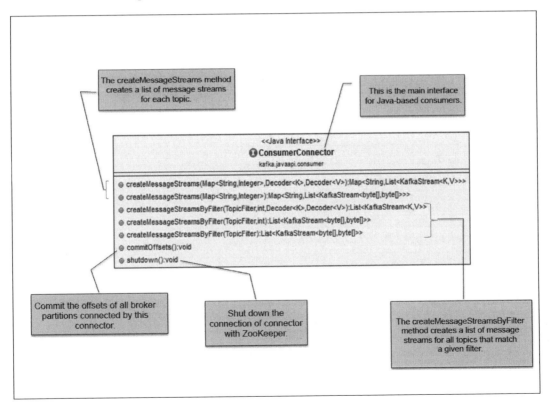

- KafkaStream: Objects of the `kafka.consumer.KafkaStream` class are returned by the `createMessageStreams` call from the `ConsumerConnector` implementation. This list of the `KafkaStream` objects is returned for each topic, which can further create an iterator over messages in the stream. The following is the Scala-based class declaration:

```
class KafkaStream[K,V] (private val queue:
                        BlockingQueue[FetchedDataChunk],
                        consumerTimeoutMs: Int,
                        private val keyDecoder: Decoder[K],
                        private val valueDecoder: Decoder[V],
                        val clientId: String)
```

Here, the parameters K and V specify the type for the partition key and message value, respectively.

In the create call from the `ConsumerConnector` class, clients can specify the number of desired streams, where each stream object is used for single-threaded processing. These stream objects may represent the merging of multiple unique partitions.

- ConsumerConfig: The `kafka.consumer.ConsumerConfig` class encapsulates the property values required for establishing the connection with ZooKeeper, such as ZooKeeper URL, ZooKeeper session timeout, and ZooKeeper sink time. It also contains the property values required by the consumer such as group ID and so on.

A high-level API-based working consumer example is discussed after the next section.

The low-level consumer API

The high-level API does not allow consumers to control interactions with brokers. Also known as "simple consumer API", the low-level consumer API is stateless and provides fine grained control over the communication between Kafka broker and the consumer. It allows consumers to set the message offset with every request raised to the broker and maintains the metadata at the consumer's end. This API can be used by both online as well as offline consumers such as Hadoop. These types of consumers can also perform multiple reads for the same message or manage transactions to ensure the message is consumed only once.

Compared to the high-level consumer API, developers need to put in extra effort to gain low-level control within consumers by keeping track of offsets, figuring out the lead broker for the topic and partition, handling lead broker changes, and so on.

In the low-level consumer API, consumers first query the live broker to find out the details about the lead broker. Information about the live broker can be passed on to the consumers either using a properties file or from the command line. The `topicsMetadata()` method of the `kafka.javaapi.TopicMetadataResponse` class is used to find out metadata about the topic of interest from the lead broker. For message partition reading, the `kafka.api.OffsetRequest` class defines two constants: `EarliestTime` and `LatestTime`, to find the beginning of the data in the logs and the new messages stream. These constants also help consumers to track which messages are already read.

The main class used within the low-level consumer API is the `SimpleConsumer` (`kafka.javaapi.consumer.SimpleConsumer`) class. The following is the class diagram for the `SimpleConsumer` class:

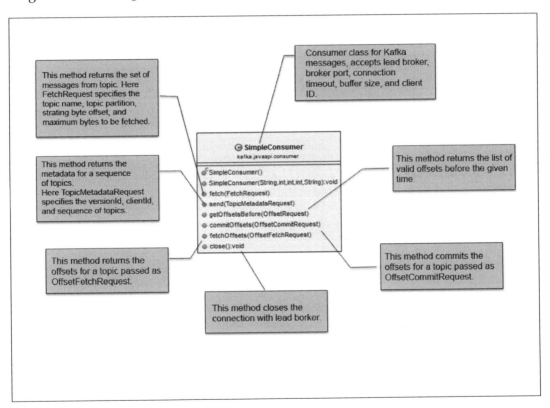

A simple consumer class provides a connection to the lead broker for fetching the messages from the topic and methods to get the topic metadata and the list of offsets.

A few more important classes for building different request objects are
FetchRequest (kafka.api.FetchRequest), OffsetRequest (kafka.javaapi.
OffsetRequest), OffsetFetchRequest (kafka.javaapi.OffsetFetchRequest),
OffsetCommitRequest (kafka.javaapi.OffsetCommitRequest), and
TopicMetadataRequest (kafka.javaapi.TopicMetadataRequest).

 All the examples in this chapter are based on the high-level
consumer API. For examples based on the low-level consumer
API, refer to https://cwiki.apache.org/confluence/
display/KAFKA/0.8.0+SimpleConsumer+Example.

Simple Java consumers

Now we will start writing a single-threaded simple Java consumer developed
using the high-level consumer API for consuming the messages from a topic.
This SimpleHLConsumer class is used to fetch a message from a specific topic and
consume it, assuming that there is a single partition within the topic.

Importing classes

As a first step, we need to import the following classes:

```
import kafka.consumer.ConsumerConfig;
import kafka.consumer.ConsumerIterator;
import kafka.consumer.KafkaStream;
import kafka.javaapi.consumer.ConsumerConnector;
```

Defining properties

As a next step, we need to define properties for making a connection with Zookeeper
and pass these properties to the Kafka consumer using the following code:

```
Properties props = new Properties();
props.put("zookeeper.connect", "localhost:2181");
props.put("group.id", "testgroup");
props.put("zookeeper.session.timeout.ms", "500");
props.put("zookeeper.sync.time.ms", "250");
props.put("auto.commit.interval.ms", "1000");
new ConsumerConfig(props);
```

Now let us see the major properties mentioned in the code:

- `zookeeper.connect`: This property specifies the ZooKeeper `<node:port>` connection detail that is used to find the Zookeeper running instance in the cluster. In the Kafka cluster, Zookeeper is used to store offsets of messages consumed for a specific topic and partition by this consumer group.

- `group.id`: This property specifies the name for the consumer group shared by all the consumers within the group. This is also the process name used by Zookeeper to store offsets.

- `zookeeper.session.timeout.ms`: This property specifies the Zookeeper session timeout in milliseconds and represents the amount of time Kafka will wait for Zookeeper to respond to a request before giving up and continuing to consume messages.

- `zookeeper.sync.time.ms`: This property specifies the ZooKeeper sync time in milliseconds between the ZooKeeper leader and the followers.

- `auto.commit.interval.ms`: This property defines the frequency in milliseconds at which consumer offsets get committed to Zookeeper.

Reading messages from a topic and printing them

As a final step, we need to read the message using the following code:

```
Map<String, Integer> topicMap = new HashMap<String, Integer>();
// 1 represents the single thread
topicCount.put(topic, new Integer(1));

Map<String, List<KafkaStream<byte[], byte[]>>> consumerStreamsMap =
consumer.createMessageStreams(topicMap);

// Get the list of message streams for each topic, using the default
decoder.
List<KafkaStream<byte[], byte[]>>streamList =  consumerStreamsMap.
get(topic);

for (final KafkaStream <byte[], byte[]> stream : streamList) {
ConsumerIterator<byte[], byte[]> consumerIte = stream.iterator();
  while (consumerIte.hasNext())
    System.out.println("Message from Single Topic :: "
    + new String(consumerIte.next().message()));
}
```

So the complete program will look like the following code:

```
package kafka.examples.ch5;

import java.util.HashMap;
import java.util.List;
import java.util.Map;
import java.util.Properties;

import kafka.consumer.ConsumerConfig;
import kafka.consumer.ConsumerIterator;
import kafka.consumer.KafkaStream;
import kafka.javaapi.consumer.ConsumerConnector;

public class SimpleHLConsumer {
  private final ConsumerConnector consumer;
  private final String topic;

  public SimpleHLConsumer(String zookeeper, String groupId, String
topic) {
    consumer = kafka.consumer.Consumer
        .createJavaConsumerConnector(createConsumerConfig(zookeeper,
            groupId));
    this.topic = topic;
  }

  private static ConsumerConfig createConsumerConfig(String zookeeper,
        String groupId) {
    Properties props = new Properties();
    props.put("zookeeper.connect", zookeeper);
    props.put("group.id", groupId);
    props.put("zookeeper.session.timeout.ms", "500");
    props.put("zookeeper.sync.time.ms", "250");
    props.put("auto.commit.interval.ms", "1000");

    return new ConsumerConfig(props);

  }

  public void testConsumer() {

    Map<String, Integer> topicMap = new HashMap<String, Integer>();
```

```
    // Define single thread for topic
    topicMap.put(topic, new Integer(1));

    Map<String, List<KafkaStream<byte[], byte[]>>> consumerStreamsMap
=
        consumer.createMessageStreams(topicMap);

    List<KafkaStream<byte[], byte[]>> streamList = consumerStreamsMap
        .get(topic);

    for (final KafkaStream<byte[], byte[]> stream : streamList) {
      ConsumerIterator<byte[], byte[]> consumerIte = stream.
iterator();
      while (consumerIte.hasNext())
        System.out.println("Message from Single Topic :: "
          + new String(consumerIte.next().message()));
    }
    if (consumer != null)
      consumer.shutdown();
  }

  public static void main(String[] args) {

    String zooKeeper = args[0];
    String groupId = args[1];
    String topic = args[2];
    SimpleHLConsumer simpleHLConsumer = new SimpleHLConsumer(
        zooKeeper, groupId, topic);
    simpleHLConsumer.testConsumer();
  }

}
```

Before running this, make sure you have created the topic `kafkatopic` from the command line:

```
[root@localhost kafka_2.9.2-0.8.1.1]#bin/kafka-topics.sh --create
--zookeeper localhost:2181 --replication-factor 1 --partitions 3 --topic
kafkatopic
```

Before compiling and running a Java-based Kafka program in the console, make sure you download the slf4j-1.7.7.tar.gz file from http://www.slf4j.org/download.html and copy slf4j-log4j12-1.7.7.jar contained within slf4j-1.7.7.tar.gz to the /opt/kafka_2.9.2-0.8.1.1/libs directory. Also add all the libraries available in /opt/kafka_2.9.2-0.8.1.1/libs to the classpath using the following commands:

```
[root@localhost kafka_2.9.2-0.8.1.1]# export KAFKA_
LIB=/opt/kafka_2.9.2-0.8.1.1/libs
[root@localhost kafka_2.9.2-0.8.1.1]# export
CLASSPATH=.:$KAFKA_LIB/jopt-simple-3.2.jar:$KAFKA_
LIB/kafka_2.9.2-0.8.1.1.jar:$KAFKA_LIB/log4j-1.2.15.
jar:$KAFKA_LIB/metrics-core-2.2.0.jar:$KAFKA_LIB/
scala-library-2.9.2.jar:$KAFKA_LIB/slf4j-api-
1.7.2.jar:$KAFKA_LIB/slf4j-log4j12-1.7.7.jar:$KAFKA_
LIB/snappy-java-1.0.5.jar:$KAFKA_LIB/zkclient-
0.3.jar:$KAFKA_LIB/zookeeper-3.3.4.jar
```

Also run the SimpleProducer class developed in *Chapter 4, Writing Producers*, which takes two arguments: first, the topic name and second, the number of messages to be published as follows:

```
[root@localhost kafka_2.9.2-0.8.1.1]# java kafka.examples.ch4.
SimpleProducer kafkatopic 100
```

Compile the preceding SimpleHLConsumer class using the following command:

```
[root@localhost kafka_2.9.2-0.8.1.1]# javac -d . kafka/examples/ch5/
SimpleHLConsumer.java
```

Run the simple high-level consumer using the following command in a separate console window:

```
[root@localhost kafka_2.9.2-0.8.1.1]# java kafka.examples.ch5.
SimpleHLConsumer localhost:2181 testgroup kafkatopic
```

For successful execution, the SimpleHLConsumer class takes three arguments: first, the Zookeeper connection string <host:port>; second, the unique group ID; and third, the Kafka topic name.

Multithreaded Java consumers

The previous example is a very basic example of a consumer that consumes messages from a single broker with no explicit partitioning of messages within the topic. Let's jump to the next level and write another program that consumes messages from multiple partitions connecting to single/multiple topics.

A multithreaded, high-level, consumer-API-based design is usually based on the number of partitions in the topic and follows a one-to-one mapping approach between the thread and the partitions within the topic. For example, if four partitions are defined for any topic, as a best practice, only four threads should be initiated with the consumer application to read the data; otherwise, some conflicting behavior, such as threads never receiving a message or a thread receiving messages from multiple partitions, may occur. Also, receiving multiple messages will not guarantee that the messages will be placed in order. For example, a thread may receive two messages from the first partition and three from the second partition, then three more from the first partition, followed by some more from the first partition, even if the second partition has data available.

Let's move further on.

Importing classes

As a first step, we need to import the following classes:

```
import kafka.consumer.ConsumerConfig;
import kafka.consumer.ConsumerIterator;
import kafka.consumer.KafkaStream;
import kafka.javaapi.consumer.ConsumerConnector;
```

Defining properties

As the next step, we need to define properties for making a connection with Zookeeper and pass these properties to the Kafka consumer using the following code:

```
Properties props = new Properties();
props.put("zookeeper.connect", "localhost:2181");
props.put("group.id", "testgroup");
props.put("zookeeper.session.timeout.ms", "500");
props.put("zookeeper.sync.time.ms", "250");
props.put("auto.commit.interval.ms", "1000");
new ConsumerConfig(props);
```

The preceding properties have already been discussed in the previous example. For more details on Kafka consumer properties, refer to the last section of this chapter.

Reading the message from threads and printing it

The only difference in this section from the previous section is that we first create a thread pool and get the Kafka streams associated with each thread within the thread pool, as shown in the following code:

```
// Define thread count for each topic
topicMap.put(topic, new Integer(threadCount));

// Here we have used a single topic but we can also add
// multiple topics to topicCount MAP
Map<String, List<KafkaStream<byte[], byte[]>>> consumerStreamsMap
        = consumer.createMessageStreams(topicMap);

List<KafkaStream<byte[], byte[]>> streamList = consumerStreamsMap.
get(topic);

// Launching the thread pool
executor = Executors.newFixedThreadPool(threadCount);
```

The complete program listing for the multithread Kafka consumer based on the Kafka high-level consumer API is as follows:

```
package kafka.examples.ch5;

import java.util.HashMap;
import java.util.List;
import java.util.Map;
import java.util.Properties;
import java.util.concurrent.ExecutorService;
import java.util.concurrent.Executors;

import kafka.consumer.ConsumerConfig;
import kafka.consumer.ConsumerIterator;
import kafka.consumer.KafkaStream;
import kafka.javaapi.consumer.ConsumerConnector;

public class MultiThreadHLConsumer {

  private ExecutorService executor;
  private final ConsumerConnector consumer;
  private final String topic;
```

```
   public MultiThreadHLConsumer(String zookeeper, String groupId,
String topic) {
       consumer = kafka.consumer.Consumer
           .createJavaConsumerConnector(createConsumerConfig(zookeeper,
groupId));
       this.topic = topic;
   }

   private static ConsumerConfig createConsumerConfig(String zookeeper,
           String groupId) {
       Properties props = new Properties();
       props.put("zookeeper.connect", zookeeper);
       props.put("group.id", groupId);
       props.put("zookeeper.session.timeout.ms", "500");
       props.put("zookeeper.sync.time.ms", "250");
       props.put("auto.commit.interval.ms", "1000");

       return new ConsumerConfig(props);

   }

   public void shutdown() {
     if (consumer != null)
       consumer.shutdown();
     if (executor != null)
       executor.shutdown();
   }

   public void testMultiThreadConsumer(int threadCount) {

       Map<String, Integer> topicMap = new HashMap<String, Integer>();

       // Define thread count for each topic
       topicMap.put(topic, new Integer(threadCount));

       // Here we have used a single topic but we can also add
       // multiple topics to topicCount MAP
       Map<String, List<KafkaStream<byte[], byte[]>>> consumerStreamsMap
=
           consumer.createMessageStreams(topicMap);

       List<KafkaStream<byte[], byte[]>> streamList = consumerStreamsMap
           .get(topic);
```

```
        // Launching the thread pool
        executor = Executors.newFixedThreadPool(threadCount);

        // Creating an object messages consumption
        int count = 0;
        for (final KafkaStream<byte[], byte[]> stream : streamList) {
          final int threadNumber = count;
          executor.submit(new Runnable() {
          public void run() {
          ConsumerIterator<byte[], byte[]> consumerIte = stream.
iterator();
            while (consumerIte.hasNext())
              System.out.println("Thread Number " + threadNumber + ": "
              + new String(consumerIte.next().message()));
              System.out.println("Shutting down Thread Number: " +
              threadNumber);
              }
          });
          count++;
        }
        if (consumer != null)
          consumer.shutdown();
        if (executor != null)
          executor.shutdown();
    }

  public static void main(String[] args) {

      String zooKeeper = args[0];
      String groupId = args[1];
      String topic = args[2];
      int threadCount = Integer.parseInt(args[3]);
      MultiThreadHLConsumer multiThreadHLConsumer =
          new MultiThreadHLConsumer(zooKeeper, groupId, topic);
      multiThreadHLConsumer.testMultiThreadConsumer(threadCount);
      try {
        Thread.sleep(10000);
      } catch (InterruptedException ie) {

      }
      multiThreadHLConsumer.shutdown();

    }
  }
```

Compile the preceding program, and before running it, read the following tip.

 Before we run this program, we need to make sure our cluster is running as a multi-broker cluster (comprising either single or multiple nodes). For more information on how to set up single node—multiple broker cluster, refer to *Chapter 2, Setting Up a Kafka Cluster.*

Once your multi-broker cluster is up, create a topic with four partitions and set the replication factor to 2 before running this program using the following command:

```
[root@localhost kafka-0.8]# bin/kafka-topics.sh --zookeeper
localhost:2181 --create --topic kafkatopic --partitions 4 --replication-
factor 2
```

Also, run the `SimpleProducer` class developed in *Chapter 4, Writing Producers,* which takes two arguments: first, the topic name and second, the number of messages to be published, as follows:

```
[root@localhost kafka_2.9.2-0.8.1.1]# java kafka.examples.ch4.
SimpleProducer kafkatopic 100
```

Compile the preceding `MultiThreadHLConsumer` class using the following command:

```
[root@localhost kafka_2.9.2-0.8.1.1]# javac -d . kafka/examples/ch5/
MultiThreadHLConsumer.java
```

Now run the multithreaded high-level consumer using the following command in a separate console window:

```
[root@localhost kafka_2.9.2-0.8.1.1]# java kafka.examples.ch5.
MultiThreadHLConsumer localhost:2181 testgroup kafkatopic 4
```

For successful execution, the `SimpleHLConsumer` class takes four arguments:

- The Zookeeper connection string `<host:port>`
- The unique group ID
- The Kafka topic name
- The thread count

This program will print all partitions of messages associated with each thread.

The Kafka consumer property list

The following lists of a few important properties that can be configured for high-level, consumer-API-based Kafka consumers. The Scala class `kafka.consumer.ConsumerConfig` provides implementation-level details for consumer configurations. For a complete list, visit `http://kafka.apache.org/documentation.html#consumerconfigs`.

Property name	Description	Default value
`group.id`	This property defines a unique identity for the set of consumers within the same consumer group.	
`consumer.id`	This property is specified for the Kafka consumer and generated automatically if not defined.	`null`
`zookeeper.connect`	This property specifies the Zookeeper connection string, `< hostname:port/chroot/path>`. Kafka uses Zookeeper to store offsets of messages consumed for a specific topic and partition by the consumer group. `/chroot/path` defines the data location in a global zookeeper namespace.	
`client.id`	The `client.id` value is specified by the Kafka client with each request and is used to identify the client making the requests.	`${group.id}`
`zookeeper.session.timeout.ms`	This property defines the time (in milliseconds) for a Kafka consumer to wait for a Zookeeper pulse before it is declared dead and rebalance is initiated.	`6000`
`zookeeper.connection.timeout.ms`	This value defines the maximum waiting time (in milliseconds) for the client to establish a connection with ZooKeeper.	`6000`
`zookeeper.sync.time.ms`	This property defines the time it takes to sync a Zookeeper follower with the Zookeeper leader (in milliseconds).	`2000`
`auto.commit.enable`	This property enables a periodical commit of message offsets to the Zookeeper that are already fetched by the consumer. In the event of consumer failures, these committed offsets are used as a starting position by the new consumers.	`true`

Property name	Description	Default value
auto.commit.interval.ms	This property defines the frequency (in milliseconds) for the consumed offsets to get committed to ZooKeeper.	60 * 1000
auto.offset.reset	This property defines the offset value if an initial offset is available in Zookeeper or the offset is out of range. Possible values are: • largest: reset to largest offset • smallest: reset to smallest offset • anything else: throw an exception	largest
consumer.timeout.ms	This property throws an exception to the consumer if no message is available for consumption after the specified interval.	-1

Summary

In this chapter, we have learned how to write basic consumers and learned about some advanced levels of Java consumers that consume messages from partitions.

In the next chapter, we will learn how to integrate Kafka with Storm and Hadoop.

6
Kafka Integrations

Consider a use case for a website where continuous security events, such as user authentication and authorization to access secure resources, need to be tracked, and decisions need to be taken in real time for any security breach. Using any typical batch-oriented data processing systems, such as Hadoop, where all the data needs to be collected first and then processed to reveal patterns, will make it too late to decide whether there is any security threat to the web application or not. Hence, this is the classical use case for real-time data processing.

Let's consider another use case, where raw clickstreams generated by customers through website usage are captured and preprocessed. Processing these clickstreams provides valuable insight into customer preferences and these insights can be coupled later with marketing campaigns and recommendation engines to offer an analysis of consumers. Hence, we can simply say that this large amount of clickstream data stored on Hadoop will get processed by Hadoop MapReduce jobs in batch mode, not in real time.

In this chapter, we shall be exploring how Kafka can be integrated with the following technologies to address different use cases, such as real-time processing using Storm, as Spark Streaming, and batch processing using Hadoop:

- Kafka integration with Storm
- Kafka integration with Hadoop

So let's start.

Kafka integration with Storm

Processing small amounts of data in real-time was never a challenge using technologies such as **Java Messaging Service (JMS)**; however, these processing systems show performance limitations when dealing with large volumes of streaming data. Also, these systems are not good horizontally scalable solutions.

Introducing Storm

Storm is an open source, distributed, reliable, and fault-tolerant system for processing streams of large volumes of data in real-time. It supports many use cases, such as real-time analytics, online machine learning, continuous computation, and the **Extract Transformation Load (ETL)** paradigm.

There are various components that work together for streaming data processing, as follows:

- **Spout**: This is a continuous stream of log data.
- **Bolt**: The spout passes the data to a component called **bolt**. A bolt consumes any number of input streams, does some processing, and possibly emits new streams. For example, emitting a stream of trend analysis by processing a stream of tweets.

The following diagram shows spout and bolt in the Storm architecture:

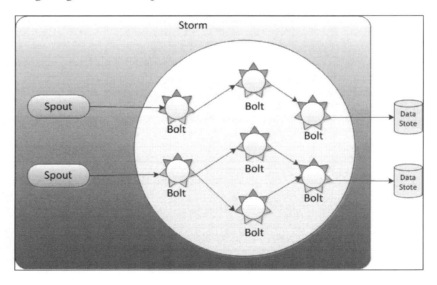

We can assume a Storm cluster to be a chain of bolt components, where each bolt performs some kind of transformation on the data streamed by the spout. Other than spout and bolts, a few other components are as follows:

- Tuple: This is the native data structure (name list values of any data type) used by Storm.

- Stream: This represents a sequence of tuples.

- Workers: These represent the Storm process.

- Executors: A Storm thread launched by a Storm worker. Here, workers may run one or more executors and executors may run one or more Storm job(s) from a spout or bolt.

Next in the Storm cluster, jobs are typically referred to as **topologies**; the only difference is that these topologies run forever. For real-time computation on Storm, topologies that are nothing but graphs of computation are created. Typically, topologies define how data will flow from spouts through bolts. These topologies can be transactional or non-transactional in nature.

Complete information about Storm can be found at
`http://storm-project.net/`.

The following section is useful if you have worked with Storm or have working knowledge of Storm.

Integrating Storm

We have already learned in the previous chapters that Kafka is a high-performance publisher-subscriber-based messaging system with highly scalable properties. Kafka spout is available for integrating Storm with Kafka clusters.

The Kafka spout is a regular spout implementation that reads the data from a Kafka cluster. This Kafka spout, which was available earlier at `https://github.com/wurstmeister/storm-kafka-0.8-plus`, is now merged into the core Storm project version 0.9.2-incubating and can be found at `https://github.com/apache/storm/tree/master/external/storm-kafka`. This storm-kafka spout provides the key features such as support for dynamic discovery of Kafka brokers and "exactly once" tuple processing. Apart from the regular Storm spout for Kafka, it also provides the Trident spout implementation for Kafka. In this section, our focus will remain on the regular storm-kafka spout.

Trident is a high-level abstraction for doing real-time computing on top of Storm. It allows us to seamlessly intermix high throughput (millions of messages per second), stateful stream processing with low-latency distributed querying. For more information https://storm.apache.org/documentation/Trident-tutorial.html.

Both spout implementations use the `BrokerHost` interface that tracks Kafka broker host-to-partition mapping and `KafkaConfig` parameters. Two implementations, `ZkHosts` and `StaticHosts`, are provided for the `BrokerHost` interface.

The `ZkHosts` implementation is used for dynamically tracking Kafka broker-to-partition mapping with the help of Kafka's zookeeper's entries:

```
public ZkHosts(String brokerZkStr, String brokerZkPath)
public ZkHosts(String brokerZkStr)
```

The preceding constructors are used to create the instance of `ZkHosts`. Here, `brokerZkStr` can be `localhost:9092` and `brokerZkPath` is the root directory under which all the topic and partition information is stored. The default value of `brokerZkPath` is `/brokers`.

The `StaticHosts` implementation is used for static partitioning information as:

```
//localhost:9092. Uses default port as 9092.
Broker brokerPartition0 = new Broker("localhost");

//localhost:9092. Takes the port explicitly
Broker brokerPartition1 = new Broker("localhost", 9092);

//localhost:9092 specified as one string.
Broker brokerPartition2 = new Broker("localhost:9092");

GlobalPartitionInformation partitionInfo = new
GlobalPartitionInformation();

//mapping form partition 0 to brokerPartition0
partitionInfo.addPartition(0, brokerPartition0);

//mapping form partition 1 to brokerPartition1
partitionInfo.addPartition(1, brokerPartition1);

//mapping form partition 2 to brokerPartition2
partitionInfo.addPartition(2, brokerPartition2);

StaticHosts hosts = new StaticHosts(partitionInfo);
```

For creating the `StaticHosts` instance, the first instance of `GlobalPartitionInformation` is created as shown in the preceding code. Next, the `KafkaConfig` instance needs to be created for constructing the Kafka spout as:

```
public KafkaConfig(BrokerHosts hosts, String topic)
public KafkaConfig(BrokerHosts hosts, String topic, String clientId)
```

The preceding constructors take the following parameters:

- A list of Kafka brokers
- The topic name used to read the message
- Client ID, used as a part of the Zookeeper path where the spout as a consumer stores the current consumption offset.

The `KafkaConfig` class also has a bunch of public variables for controlling the application's behavior and how spout fetches messages from the Kafka cluster:

```
public int fetchSizeBytes = 1024 * 1024;
public int socketTimeoutMs = 10000;
public int fetchMaxWait = 10000;
public int bufferSizeBytes = 1024 * 1024;
public MultiScheme scheme = new RawMultiScheme();
public boolean forceFromStart = false;
public long startOffsetTime =
      kafka.api.OffsetRequest.EarliestTime();
public long maxOffsetBehind = Long.MAX_VALUE;
public boolean useStartOffsetTimeIfOffsetOutOfRange = true;
public int metricsTimeBucketSizeInSecs = 60;
```

The `Spoutconfig` class extends the `KafkaConfig` class to support two additional values as `zkroot` and `id`:

```
public SpoutConfig(BrokerHosts hosts, String topic, String zkRoot,
String id);
```

The preceding constructor additionally takes the following:

- The root path in Zookeeper, where spout stores the consumer offset
- The unique identity of the spout

The following code sample shows the `KafkaSpout` class instance initialization with the previous parameters:

```
// Creating instance for BrokerHosts interface implementation
BrokerHosts hosts = new ZkHosts(brokerZkConnString);
```

```
// Creating instance of SpoutConfig
SpoutConfig spoutConfig = new SpoutConfig(brokerHosts, topicName, "/"
+ topicName, UUID.randomUUID().toString());

// Defines how the byte[] consumed from kafka gets transformed into //
a storm tuple
spoutConfig.scheme = new SchemeAsMultiScheme(new StringScheme());

// Creating instance of KafkaSpout
KafkaSpout kafkaSpout = new KafkaSpout(spoutConfig);
```

The following diagram shows the high-level integration view of what a Kafka Storm working model will look like:

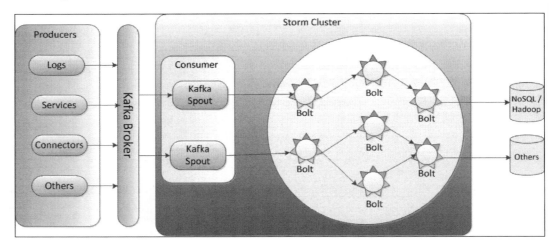

The Kafka spout uses the same Zookeeper instance that is used by Apache Storm, to store the states of the message offset and segment consumption tracking if it is consumed. These offsets are stored at the root path specified for the Zookeeper. The Kafka spout uses these offsets to replay tuples in the event of a downstream failure or timeout. Although it also has a provision to rewind to a previous offset rather than starting from the last saved offset, Kafka chooses the latest offset written around the specified timestamp:

```
spoutConfig.forceStartOffsetTime(TIMESTAMP);
```

Here the value -1 forces the Kafka spout to restart from the latest offset and -2 forces the spout to restart from the earliest offset.

This storm-kafka spout also has a as it has no support for Kafka 0.7x brokers and only supports Kafka 0.8.1.x onwards.

To run Kafka with Storm, clusters for both Storm and Kafka need to be set up and should be running. A Storm cluster setup is beyond the scope of this book.

Kafka integration with Hadoop

Resource sharing, stability, availability, and scalability are a few of the many challenges of distributed computing. Nowadays, an additional challenge is to process extremely large volumes of data in TBs or PBs.

Introducing Hadoop

Hadoop is a large-scale distributed batch-processing framework that parallelizes data processing across many nodes and addresses the challenges for distributed computing, including big data.

Hadoop works on the principle of the MapReduce framework (introduced by Google), which provides a simple interface for the parallelization and distribution of large-scale computations. Hadoop has its own distributed data filesystem called **Hadoop Distributed File System** (**HDFS**). In any typical Hadoop cluster, HDFS splits the data into small pieces (called **blocks**) and distributes it to all the nodes. HDFS also replicates these small pieces of data and stores them to make sure that, if any node is down, the data is available from another node.

The following diagram shows the high-level view of a multi-node Hadoop cluster:

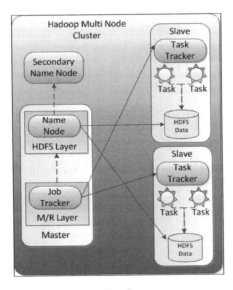

Hadoop has the following main components:

- **Name node**: This is a single point of interaction for HDFS. A name node stores information about the small pieces (blocks) of data that are distributed across the node.

- **Secondary name node**: This node stores edit logs, which are helpful to for restoring the latest updated state of HDFS in the case of a name node failure.

- **Data node**: These nodes store the actual data distributed by the name node in blocks and also store the replicated copy of data from other nodes.

- **Job tracker**: This is responsible for splitting the MapReduce jobs into smaller tasks.

- **Task tracker**: The task tracker is responsible for the execution of tasks split by the job tracker.

The data nodes and the task tracker share the same machines and the MapReduce job split; execution of tasks is done based on the data store location information provided by the name node.

Now before we discuss the Kafka integration with Hadoop let's quickly set up a single node Hadoop cluster in pseudo distributed mode.

Hadoop clusters can be set up in three different modes:
- Local mode
- Pseudo distributed mode
- Fully distributed mode

Local mode and pseudo distributed mode work on single-node cluster. In local mode, all the Hadoop main components run in the single JVM instance; whereas, in pseudo distributed mode, each component runs in a separate JVM instance on the single node. Pseudo distributed mode is primarily used as a development environment by developers. In fully distributed mode, all the components run on separate nodes and are used in test and production environments.

The following are the steps used for creating pseudo distributed mode cluster:

1. Install and configure Java. Refer to the *Installing Java 1.7 or higher* section in *Chapter 1, Introducing Kafka*.

2. Download the current stable Hadoop distribution from `http://www.apache.org/dyn/closer.cgi/hadoop/common/`.

3. Unpack the downloaded Hadoop distribution in /opt and add Hadoop's bin directory to the path as:

    ```
    # Assuming your installation directory is /opt/Hadoop-2.6.0
    [root@localhost opt]#export HADOOP_HOME=/opt/hadoop-2.6.0
    [root@localhost opt]#export PATH=$PATH:$HADOOP_HOME/bin
    ```

4. Add the following configurations:

    ```
    etc/hadoop/core-site.xml:
    <configuration>
        <property>
            <name>fs.defaultFS</name>
            <value>hdfs://localhost:9000</value>
        </property>
    </configuration>

     etc/hadoop/hdfs-site.xml:
    <configuration>
        <property>
            <name>dfs.replication</name>
            <value>1</value>
        </property>
    </configuration>
    ```

5. Set up ssh to the localhost without a passphrase:

    ```
    [root@localhost opt]# ssh localhost
    ```

    If ssh-to-localhost does not work without a passphrase, execute the following commands:

    ```
    [root@localhost opt]# ssh-keygen -t dsa -P '' -f ~/.ssh/id_dsa
    [root@localhost opt]# cat ~/.ssh/id_dsa.pub >> ~/.ssh/authorized_keys
    ```

6. Format the filesystem:

    ```
    [root@localhost opt]# bin/hdfs namenode -format
    ```

7. Start the NameNode daemon and DataNode daemon:

    ```
    [root@localhost opt]# sbin/start-dfs.sh
    ```

Once the Hadoop cluster is set up successfully, browse the web interface for the NameNode at http://localhost:50070/.

Integrating Hadoop

This section is useful if you have worked with Hadoop or have a working knowledge of Hadoop.

For real-time publish-subscribe use cases, Kafka is used to build a pipeline that is available for real-time processing or monitoring and to load the data into Hadoop, NoSQL, or data warehousing systems for offline processing and reporting.

Kafka provides the source code for both the Hadoop producer and consumer, under its `contrib` directory.

Hadoop producers

A Hadoop producer provides a bridge for publishing the data from a Hadoop cluster to Kafka, as shown in the following diagram:

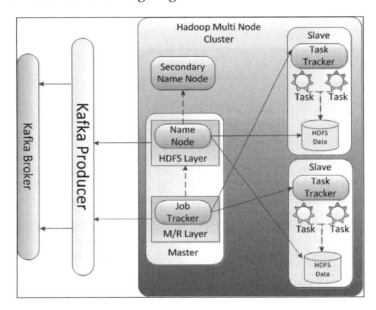

For a Kafka producer, Kafka topics are considered as URIs and, to connect to a specific Kafka broker, URIs are specified as follows:

```
kafka://<kafka-broker>/<kafka-topic>
```

The Hadoop producer code suggests two possible approaches for getting the data from Hadoop:

- **Using the Pig script and writing messages in Avro format**: In this approach, Kafka producers use Pig scripts for writing data in a binary Avro format, where each row signifies a single message. For pushing the data into the Kafka cluster, the `AvroKafkaStorage` class (it extends Pig's `StoreFunc` class) takes the Avro schema as its first argument and connects to the Kafka URI. Using the `AvroKafkaStorage` producer, we can also easily write to multiple topics and brokers in the same Pig-script-based job. While writing Pig scripts, required Kafka JAR files also need to be registered. The following is the sample Pig script:

  ```
  REGISTER hadoop-producer_2.8.0-0.8.0.jar;
  REGISTER avro-1.4.0.jar;
  REGISTER piggybank.jar;
  REGISTER kafka-0.8.0.jar;
  REGISTER jackson-core-asl-1.5.5.jar;
  REGISTER jackson-mapper-asl-1.5.5.jar;
  REGISTER scala-library.jar;

  member_info = LOAD 'member_info.tsv' AS (member_id : int, name :
  chararray);

  names = FOREACH member_info GENERATE name;

  STORE member_info INTO 'kafka://localhost:9092/member_info' USING
  kafka.bridge.AvroKafkaStorage('"string"');
  ```

  In the preceding script, the Pig `StoreFunc` class makes use of `AvroStorage` in Piggybank to convert from Pig's data model to the specified Avro schema.

- **Using the Kafka OutputFormat class for jobs**: In this approach, the Kafka `OutputFormat` class (it extends Hadoop's `OutputFormat` class) is used for publishing data to the Kafka cluster. Using the 0.20 MapReduce API, this approach publishes messages as bytes and provides control over output by using low-level methods of publishing. The Kafka `OutputFormat` class uses the `KafkaRecordWriter` class (it extends Hadoop's `RecordWriter` class) for writing a record (message) to a Hadoop cluster.

For Kafka producers, we can also configure Kafka producer parameters by prefixing them with `kafka.output` in the job configuration. For example, to change the compression codec, add the `kafka.output.compression.codec` parameter (for example, `SET kafka.output.compression.codec 0` in Pig script for no compression). Along with these values, Kafka broker information (`kafka.metadata.broker.list`), the topic (`kafka.output.topic`), and the schema (`kafka.output.schema`) are injected into the job's configuration.

Hadoop consumers

A Hadoop consumer is a Hadoop job that pulls data from the Kafka broker and pushes it into HDFS. The following diagram shows the position of a Kafka consumer in the architecture pattern:

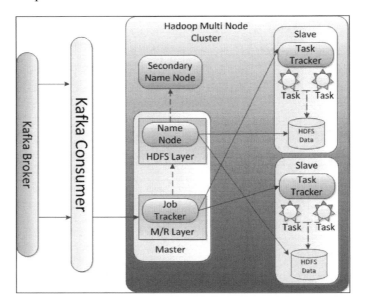

A Hadoop job performs parallel loading from Kafka to HDFS, and the number of mappers for loading the data depends on the number of files in the input directory. The output directory contains data coming from Kafka and the updated topic offsets. Individual mappers write the offset of the last consumed message to HDFS at the end of the map task. If a job fails and jobs get restarted, each mapper simply restarts from the offsets stored in HDFS.

The ETL example provided in the `Kafka-0.8.1.1-src/contrib/hadoop-consumer` directory demonstrates the extraction of Kafka data and loading it to HDFS. It requires the following inputs from a configuration file, for example, `test/test.properties`:

- `kafka.etl.topic`: The topic to be fetched.
- `kafka.server.uri`: The Kafka server URI.
- `input`: Input directory containing topic offsets that can be generated by `DataGenerator`. The number of files in this directory determines the number of mappers in the Hadoop job.
- `output`: Output directory containing Kafka data and updated topic offsets.
- `kafka.request.limit`: It is used to limit the number events fetched.

In the Kafka consumer, the `KafkaETLRecordReader` instance is a record reader associated with `KafkaETLInputFormat`. It fetches Kafka data from the server starting from the provided offsets (specified by `input`) and stops when it reaches the largest available offsets or the specified limit (specified by `kafka.request.limit`). `KafkaETLJob` also contains some helper functions to initialize job configuration and `SimpleKafkaETLJob` sets up job properties and submits the Hadoop job. Once the job is started `SimpleKafkaETLMapper` dumps Kafka data into HDFS (specified by `output`).

Summary

In this chapter, we have primarily learned how Kafka can be integrated with existing open source frameworks in the area of real-time/batch data processing. In the real-time data processing area, Kafka is integrated with Storm using the existing Storm spout. As for batch data processing, Kafka brings Hadoop-based data producers and consumes, so that data can be published onto the HDFS, processed using MapReduce, and later consumed.

In the next chapter, which is also the last chapter of this book, we will look at some of the other important facts about Kafka.

7
Operationalizing Kafka

In this last chapter, we will be exploring tools available for Kafka cluster administration and Kafka topic administration. Additionally, we will also be discussing in brief Kafka cluster mirroring and Kafka's integration with third-party tools.

The main focus areas for this chapter are as follows:

- Kafka administration tools
- Kafka cluster mirroring
- Integration with other tools

Kafka administration tools

There are a number of tools or utilities provided by Kafka 0.8.x to administrate features such as cluster management, topic tools, cluster mirroring, and so on. Let's have a quick look at these tools.

Kafka cluster tools

Cluster management is one of the prime responsibilities of the Kafka administrator. Once the cluster is started successfully, it needs to be maintained for activities such as server shutdown, leader balancing, replication, cluster mirroring, and expanding Kafka clusters. Let's talk about these in detail.

As we have learned from Kafka's design, in replication multiple partitions can have replicated data, and out of these multiple replicas, one replica acts as a lead, and the rest of the replicas act as in-sync followers of the lead replica. In the event of non-availability of a lead replica, maybe due to broker shutdown, a new lead replica needs to be selected.

For scenarios such as shutting down the Kafka broker for maintenance activity, election of the new leader is done sequentially, and this causes significant read/write operations for Zookeeper. In any big cluster with many topics/partitions, sequential election of lead replicas causes delay in availability.

To ensure high availability, Kafka provides tools for a controlled shutdown of Kafka brokers. If the broker has the lead partition shut down, this tool transfers the leadership proactively to other in-sync replicas on another broker. If there is no in-sync replica available, the tool will fail to shut down the broker in order to ensure no data is lost.

The following is the format for using this tool:

```
[root@localhost kafka_2.9.2-0.8.1.1]# bin/kafka-run-class.sh kafka.admin.
ShutdownBroker --zookeeper <zookeeper_host:port/namespace> --broker
<brokerID> --num.retries 3 --retry.interval.ms 100
```

The ZooKeeper host and the broker ID that need to be shut down are mandatory parameters. We can also specify optional parameters, the number of retries (`--num. retries`, `default value 0`) and the retry interval in milliseconds (`--retry. interval.ms`, `default value 1000`) with a controlled shutdown tool.

When a server is stopped gracefully, it will sync all its logs automatically to disk to avoid any log recovery whenever it is restarted again, as log recovery is a time-consuming activity. Before shutting down, it also migrates the leader partitions on the server to other replicas. This ensures minimal downtime for each partition (up to a few milliseconds). Controlled shutdown of a server also needs to be enabled as follows:

```
controlled.shutdown.enable=true
```

Next, in any big Kafka cluster with many brokers, topics, and partitions, Kafka ensures that the preferred/lead replicas for partitions are equally distributed among the brokers. However, if a shutdown (controlled as well) or broker failure happens, this equal distribution of lead replicas might get imbalanced within the cluster.

Kafka provides a tool that is used to maintain a balanced distribution of lead replicas within the Kafka cluster across available brokers.

The following is the format for using this tool:

```
[root@localhost kafka_2.9.2-0.8.1.1]# bin/kafka-preferred-replica-
election.sh --zookeeper <zookeeper_host:port/namespace>
```

This tool updates the ZooKeeper path with the list of topic partitions whose leader needs to be moved to the preferred replica list. Once the list is updated, the controller retrieves the list of preferred topic partitions from ZooKeeper asynchronously and, for each topic partition, controller verifies whether the preferred replica is the leader. If controller finds that the preferred replica is not the leader and is not present in the ISR list, it raises a request to the broker to make the preferred replica the leader for the partition to create a balanced distribution. If the preferred replica is not in the ISR list, the controller fails the operation to avoid any data loss. For this tool, the list of topic partitions in a JSON file format can also be provided as follows:

```
[root@localhost kafka_2.9.2-0.8.1.1]# bin/kafka-preferred-replica-
election.sh --zookeeper <zookeeper_host:port/namespace> --path-to-json-
file topicPartitionList.json
```

The following is the format of the topicPartitionList.json file:

```
{
  "partitions":
  [
    {"topic": "Kafkatopic", "partition": "0"},
    {"topic": "Kafkatopic", "partition": "1"},
    {"topic": "Kafkatopic", "partition": "2"},

    {"topic": "Kafkatopic1", "partition": "0"},
    {"topic": "Kafkatopic1", "partition": "1"},
    {"topic": "Kafkatopic1", "partition": "2"},
  ]
}
```

Adding servers

In order to add servers to a Kafka cluster, a unique broker ID needs to be assigned to the new server to set up/start Kafka on the new servers. This way of adding a new server does not automatically assign any data partitions. Hence, a newly added server will not perform any work unless existing partitions are migrated to the server or new topics are created.

The migration process for existing partitions is initiated manually by the Kafka administrator, as admin has to find out which topics or partitions should be moved. Once the partitions are identified by the administrator, the partition reassignment tool (`bin/kafka-reassign-partitions.sh`) is used to move partitions across brokers, which takes care of everything. As a migration process, Kafka will make this newly added server a follower of the partition it is migrating. This allows the new server to fully replicate the existing data in that partition. Once the new server has fully replicated the partition's contents and has become a part of the in-sync replica, one of the existing replicas will delete the partition's data. The partition reassignment tool (`kafka-reassign-partitions.sh`) runs in three different modes:

- `--generate`: In this mode, the tool generates a candidate reassignment to move all partitions of the specified topics to the new server based on the list of topics and brokers shared with the tool

- `--execute`: In this mode, the tool starts the reassignment of partitions based on the user-provided reassignment plan specified with the `--reassignment-json-file` option

- `--verify`: In this mode, the tool verifies the status (completed successfully/failed/in progress) of the reassignment for all partitions listed during the last `--execute`

The partition reassignment tool can be used to move selected topics from the current set of brokers to newly added brokers (servers). Administrator should provide a list of topics to be moved to the new server and a target list of new broker IDs. This tool evenly distributes all partitions of a given topic across the new brokers and also moves the replicas for all partitions for the input list of topics.

```
[root@localhost kafka_2.9.2-0.8.1.1]# cat topics-for-new-server.json
{"partitions":

              [{"topic": "kafkatopic",
              {"topic": "kafkatopic1"}],

   "version":1
}
```

```
[root@localhost kafka_2.9.2-0.8.1.1]# bin/kafka-reassign-partitions.sh
--zookeeper localhost:2181

--topics-to-move-json-file topics-for-new-server.json --broker-list "4,5"
--generate new-topic-reassignment.json
```

The preceding command generates the assignment (`new-topic-reassignment.json`) plan to move all partitions for topics `kafkatopic` and `kafkatopic1` to the new set of brokers having IDs 4 and 5. At the end of this move, all partitions for topics `foo1` and `foo2` will only exist on brokers 5 and 6. To initiate the assignment, the `kafka-reassign-partitions.sh` tool is used:

```
[root@localhost kafka_2.9.2-0.8.1.1]# bin/kafka-reassign-partitions.
sh --zookeeper localhost:2181 --reassignment-json-file new-topic-
reassignment.json --execute
```

This tool can also be used to selectively move the partitions from the existing broker to the new broker:

```
[root@localhost kafka_2.9.2-0.8.1.1]# cat partitions-reassignment.json

{"partitions":

            [{"topic": "kafkatopic",
              "partition": 1,
              "replicas": [1,2,4] }],
            }],

   "version":1

}
```

```
[root@localhost kafka_2.9.2-0.8.1.1]# bin/kafka-reassign-partitions.sh
--zookeeper localhost:2181

   --reassignment-json-file partitions-reassignment.json --execute
```

The preceding command selectively moves some replicas for certain partitions to the new server. Once the reassignment is done, the operation can be verified:

```
[root@localhost kafka_2.9.2-0.8.1.1]# bin/kafka-reassign-partitions.
sh --zookeeper localhost:2181 --reassignment-json-file new-topic-
reassignment.json --verify
```

```
Status of partition reassignment:
Reassignment of partition [kafkatopic,0] completed successfully
Reassignment of partition [kafkatopic,1] is in progress
Reassignment of partition [kafkatopic,2] completed successfully
Reassignment of partition [kafkatopic1,0] completed successfully
Reassignment of partition [kafkatopic1,1] completed successfully
Reassignment of partition [kafkatopic1,2] is in progress
```

To decommission any server from the Kafka cluster, the admin has to move the replica for all partitions hosted on the broker (server) to be decommissioned, to the remaining brokers with even distribution. The `kafka-reassign-partitions.sh` tool can also be used to increase the replication factor of the partition as follows:

```
[root@localhost kafka_2.9.2-0.8.1.1]# cat increase-replication-factor.
json
{"partitions":[{"topic":"kafkatopic","partition":0,"replicas":[2,3]}],
  "version":1
}


[root@localhost kafka_2.9.2-0.8.1.1]# bin/kafka-reassign-partitions.sh
--zookeeper localhost:2181
 --reassignment-json-file increase-replication-factor.json --execute
```

The preceding command assumes that partition 0 of the `kafkatopic` topic has replication factor 1 that existed on broker 2; and now it increases the replication factor from 1 to 2 and also creates the new replica on broker 3.

Kafka topic tools

By default, Kafka creates topics with a default number of partitions and replication factors (the default value is 1 for both). But, in real-life scenarios, we may need to define the number of partitions and replication factors more than once.

The following is the command to create a topic with specific parameters:

```
[root@localhost kafka_2.9.2-0.8.1.1]# bin/kafka-topics.sh --create
--zookeeper localhost:2181/chroot --replication-factor 3 --partitions 10
--topic kafkatopic
```

In the preceding command, the replication factor controls how many servers will replicate each message published by the message producer. For example, replication factor 3 means that up to two servers can fail before access is lost to the data. The partition count that enables parallelism for consumers reflects the number of logs the topic will be sharded into. Here, each partition must fit entirely on a single server. For example, if 10 partitions are defined for a topic, the full data set will be handled by no more than 10 servers excluding replicas.

The Kafka topic utility `kafka-topics.sh` can also be used to alter the Kafka topic as follows:

```
[root@localhost kafka_2.9.2-0.8.1.1]# bin/kafka-topics.sh --alter
--zookeeper localhost:2181/chroot --partitions 20 --topic kafkatopic
```

In the preceding command, 10 more partitions are added to the Kafka topic created in the previous example. Currently Kafka does not support reducing the number of partitions or changing the replication factor for topics. To delete the Kafka topic, the following command is used:

```
[root@localhost kafka_2.9.2-0.8.1.1]# bin/kafka-topics.sh --delete
--zookeeper localhost:2181/chroot --topic kafkatopic
```

Using the `kafka-topics.sh` Kafka topic utility, configuration can also be added to the Kafka topic as follows:

```
[root@localhost kafka_2.9.2-0.8.1.1]# bin/kafka-topics.sh --alter
--zookeeper localhost:2181/chroot --topic kafkatopic --config
<key>=<value>
```

To remove configuration from the Kafka topic, use the following command:

```
[root@localhost kafka_2.9.2-0.8.1.1]# bin/kafka-topics.sh --alter
--zookeeper localhost:2181/chroot --topic kafkatopic --deleteconfig
<key>=<value>
```

Kafka also provides a utility to search for the list of topics within the Kafka server. The List Topic tool provides a listing of topics and information about their partitions, replicas, or leaders by querying Zookeeper.

The following command obtains a list of topics:

```
[root@localhost kafka_2.9.2-0.8.1.1]# bin/kafka-topics.sh --list
--zookeeper localhost:2181
```

On execution of the preceding command, you should get the output shown in the following screenshot:

```
[2013-08-28 10:26:53,437] INFO Client environment:os.version=2.6.18-348.6.1.el5 (org.apache.zookeeper.ZooKeeper)
[2013-08-28 10:26:53,437] INFO Client environment:user.name=root (org.apache.zookeeper.ZooKeeper)
[2013-08-28 10:26:53,437] INFO Client environment:user.home=/root (org.apache.zookeeper.ZooKeeper)
[2013-08-28 10:26:53,437] INFO Client environment:user.dir=/opt/kafka-0.8_OLD (org.apache.zookeeper.ZooKeeper)
[2013-08-28 10:26:53,438] INFO Initiating client connection, connectString=localhost:2181 sessionTimeout=30000 watcher=org.I0Itec.zkclient.ZkClient@788ab708 (org.apache.zookeeper.ZooKeeper)
[2013-08-28 10:26:53,464] INFO Starting ZkClient event thread. (org.I0Itec.zkclient.ZkEventThread)
[2013-08-28 10:26:53,474] INFO Opening socket connection to server localhost/127.0.0.1:2181 (org.apache.zookeeper.ClientCnxn)
[2013-08-28 10:26:53,494] INFO Socket connection established to localhost/127.0.0.1:2181, initiating session (org.apache.zookeeper.ClientCnxn)
[2013-08-28 10:26:53,520] INFO Session establishment complete on server localhost/127.0.0.1:2181, sessionid = 0x140c5ef3917000b, negotiated timeout = 30000 (org.apache.zookeeper.ClientCnxn)
[2013-08-28 10:26:53,525] INFO zookeeper state changed (SyncConnected) (org.I0Itec.zkclient.ZkClient)
topic: kafkatopic       partition: 0    leader: 1    replicas: 2,3,1 isr: 1,2
topic: kafkatopic       partition: 1    leader: 1    replicas: 3,1,2 isr: 1,2
topic: othertopic       partition: 0    leader: 2    replicas: 2,1   isr: 2,1
[2013-08-28 10:26:54,325] INFO Terminate ZkClient event thread. (org.I0Itec.zkclient.ZkEventThread)
[2013-08-28 10:26:54,341] INFO EventThread shut down (org.apache.zookeeper.ClientCnxn)
[2013-08-28 10:26:54,341] INFO Session: 0x140c5ef3917000b closed (org.apache.zookeeper.ZooKeeper)
[root@localhost kafka-0.8]#
```

The preceding console output shows that we can get information about the topic and partitions that have replicated data. The output from the previous screenshot can be explained as follows:

- `leader`: This is a randomly selected node for a specific portion of the partitions and is responsible for all reads and writes for this partition
- `replicas`: This represents the list of nodes that holds the log for a specified partition
- `isr`: This represents the subset of the in-sync replicas' list that is currently alive and in sync with the leader

Note that `kafkatopic` has two partitions (partitions `0` and `1`) with three replications, whereas `othertopic` has just one partition with two replications.

While getting a list of Kafka topics, two optional arguments can also be provided as: `under-replicated-partitions` and `unavailable-partitions`. The `under-replicated-partitions` argument is used to get details of those topics/partitions that have replicas that are under-replicated. The `unavailable-partitions` argument is used to get details of those topics/partitions whose leader is not available.

Kafka cluster mirroring

The Kafka mirroring feature is used to create a replication of an existing cluster—for example, replicating an active datacenter into a passive datacenter. Kafka provides a mirror maker tool for mirroring the source cluster into a target cluster.

The following diagram depicts the mirroring tool placement in architectural form:

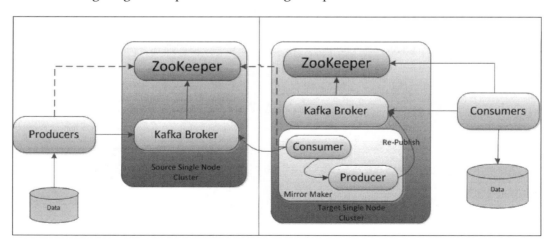

In this architecture, the job of the mirror tool is to consume the messages from the source cluster and republish them on the target cluster using the embedded producer. A similar approach is used by the Kafka migration tool to migrate from the 0.7.x Kafka cluster to the 0.8.x Kafka cluster.

To mirror the source cluster, bring up the target cluster and start the MirrorMaker processes as follows:

```
[root@localhost kafka_2.9.2-0.8.1.1]# bin/kafka-run-class.sh kafka.tools.
MirrorMaker --consumer.config sourceClusterConsumer.config --num.streams
2 --producer.config targetClusterProducer.config --whitelist=".*"
```

The minimum parameters required to start the MirrorMaker tool successfully are one or more consumer configurations, a producer configuration, and either a whitelist or a blacklist as standard Java regex patterns—for example, mirroring two topics named A and B using --whitelist 'A|B' or mirroring all topics using --whitelist '*'. The --blacklist configuration can also be used as standard Java regex patterns to specify what to exclude while mirroring. It also requires the consumer of the mirror tool to connect to the source cluster's ZooKeeper, the producer to the mirror cluster's ZooKeeper, or the broker.list parameter.

For high throughput, an asynchronous embedded producer configured in blocking mode is used. This ensures that messages will not be lost and the blocking producer will wait till the messages are written to the target cluster if the producer's queue is full. The producer's queue being full consistently indicates that the MirrorMaker is bottle-necked on republishing messages to the target mirror cluster and/or flushing messages to disk. The --num.producers option can also be used to represent a producer pool in the MirrorMaker to increase throughput as multiple producer requests can be handled by multiple consumption streams of the target cluster. The --num.streams option specifies the number of mirror consumer threads to create.

Mirroring is often used in cross data center scenarios and, in general, a high value is used for the socket buffer size (socket.buffersize) on the MirrorMaker's consumer configuration and socket.send.buffer on the source cluster broker configuration. Also, the MirrorMaker consumer's fetch size (fetch.size) should be higher than the consumer's socket buffer size. If broker.list is used in the producer configuration along with the hardware load balancer, configuration for the number of retry attempts on producer failures can also be provided.

Kafka also provides tools to check the position of the consumer while mirroring or in general. This tool shows the position of all the consumers in a consumer group and how far behind the end of the log consumers are; it indicates how well cluster mirroring is performing. This tool can be used as follows:

```
[root@localhost kafka_2.9.2-0.8.1.1]#bin/kafka-run-class.sh kafka.tools.
ConsumerOffsetChecker --group MirrorGroup --zkconnect localhost:2181
--topic kafkatopic
```

Group	Topic	Pid	Offset	logSize	Lag	Owner
MirrorGroup	kafkatopic	0	5	5	0	none
MirrorGroup	kafkatopic	1	3	4	1	none
MirrorGroup	kafkatopic	2	6	9	3	none

Here the `--zkconnect` argument points to the source cluster's ZooKeeper (for example, the source data center). The `--topic` parameter is an optional parameter and, if the topic is not specified, then the tool prints information for all topics under the specified consumer group.

Integration with other tools

This section discusses the contributions by many contributors providing integration with Apache Kafka for various needs such as logging, packaging, cloud integration, and Hadoop integration.

Camus (`https://github.com/linkedin/camus`) which provides a pipeline from Kafka to HDFS. Under this project, a single MapReduce job performs the following steps to load data to HDFS in a distributed manner:

1. As a first step, it discovers the latest topics and partition offsets from ZooKeeper.

2. Each task in the MapReduce job fetches events from the Kafka broker and commits the pulled data along with the audit count to the output folders.

3. After the completion of the job, final offsets are written to HDFS and can be further consumed by subsequent MapReduce jobs.

4. Information about the consumed messages is also updated in the Kafka cluster.

Some other useful contributions are:

- Automated deployment and configuration of Kafka and ZooKeeper on Amazon (`https://github.com/nathanmarz/kafka-deploy`)

- A logging utility (`https://github.com/leandrosilva/klogd2`)

- A REST service for Mozilla Metrics (`https://github.com/mozilla-metrics/bagheera`)

- Apache Camel-Kafka integration (`https://github.com/BreizhBeans/camel-kafka/wiki`)

> For a detailed list of Kafka ecosystem tools, please refer to `https://cwiki.apache.org/confluence/display/KAFKA/Ecosystem`.

Summary

In this chapter, we have added some more information about Kafka, such as its administrator tools, its integration, and Kafka non-Java clients.

During this complete journey through Apache Kafka, we have touched upon many important facts about Kafka. You have learned the reason why Kafka was developed, its installation procedures, and its support for different types of clusters. We also explored the Kafka's design approach, and wrote a few basic producers and consumers.

Finally, we discussed Kafka's integration with technologies such as Hadoop and Storm.

The journey of evolution never ends.

Index

synchronous replication 32

S

simple Java-based producer
about 38
classes, importing 38
message, building 39-42
message, sending 39-42
properties, defining 38
simple Java consumer
about 54
classes, importing 54
messages, reading from topic 55-58
properties, defining 54, 55
single node-multiple broker cluster
about 20
consumer, starting to consume messages 22
Kafka broker, starting 20
Kafka topic, creating 21
producer, starting to send messages 21
ZooKeeper, starting 20
single node-single broker cluster
about 14
consumer, starting to consume messages 19
Kafka broker, starting 15
Kafka topic, creating 16
producer, starting to send messages 17-19
ZooKeeper server, starting 14
Snappy 30
spout 68
Square
URL 9
Storm
about 68, 69
integrating 69-72
Kafka integration 68
URL 69

Storm architecture
bolt 68
executors 69
spout 68
tuple 69
workers 69
synchronous replication 32

T

topic 13
topicsMetadata() method 53
topologies 69
Trident
about 70
URL 70
Twitter
URL 9

U

use cases, Kafka
click streams tracking 9
commit logs 9
log aggregation 8
messaging 9
stream processing 9

Z

ZooKeeper
about 13
URL 13, 15
**zookeeper.connection.timeout.ms
property 64**
zookeeper.connect property 23, 64
zookeeper.session.timeout.ms property 64
zookeeper.sync.time.ms property 64

Thank you for buying
Learning Apache Kafka
Second Edition

About Packt Publishing

Packt, pronounced 'packed', published its first book, *Mastering phpMyAdmin for Effective MySQL Management*, in April 2004, and subsequently continued to specialize in publishing highly focused books on specific technologies and solutions.

Our books and publications share the experiences of your fellow IT professionals in adapting and customizing today's systems, applications, and frameworks. Our solution-based books give you the knowledge and power to customize the software and technologies you're using to get the job done. Packt books are more specific and less general than the IT books you have seen in the past. Our unique business model allows us to bring you more focused information, giving you more of what you need to know, and less of what you don't.

Packt is a modern yet unique publishing company that focuses on producing quality, cutting-edge books for communities of developers, administrators, and newbies alike. For more information, please visit our website at www.packtpub.com.

About Packt Open Source

In 2010, Packt launched two new brands, Packt Open Source and Packt Enterprise, in order to continue its focus on specialization. This book is part of the Packt Open Source brand, home to books published on software built around open source licenses, and offering information to anybody from advanced developers to budding web designers. The Open Source brand also runs Packt's Open Source Royalty Scheme, by which Packt gives a royalty to each open source project about whose software a book is sold.

Writing for Packt

We welcome all inquiries from people who are interested in authoring. Book proposals should be sent to author@packtpub.com. If your book idea is still at an early stage and you would like to discuss it first before writing a formal book proposal, then please contact us; one of our commissioning editors will get in touch with you.

We're not just looking for published authors; if you have strong technical skills but no writing experience, our experienced editors can help you develop a writing career, or simply get some additional reward for your expertise.

Learning Storm

ISBN: 978-1-78398-132-8   Paperback: 252 pages

Create real-time stream processing applications with Apache Storm

1. Integrate Storm with other Big Data technologies like Hadoop, HBase, and Apache Kafka.

2. Explore log processing and machine learning using Storm.

3. Step-by-step and easy-to-understand guide to effortlessly create applications with Storm.

Akka Essentials

ISBN: 978-1-84951-828-4   Paperback: 334 pages

A practical, step-by-step guide to learn and build Akka's actor-based, distributed, concurrent, and scalable Java applications

1. Build large, distributed, concurrent, and scalable applications using the Akka's Actor model.

2. Simple and clear analogy to Java/JEE application development world to explain the concepts.

3. Each chapter will teach you a concept by explaining it with clear and lucid examples– each chapter can be read independently.

Please check **www.PacktPub.com** for information on our titles

Web App Testing Using Knockout.JS

ISBN: 978-1-78398-284-4   Paperback: 154 pages

Design, implement, and maintain a fully tested JavaScript web application using Knockout.JS

1. Test JavaScript web applications using one of the most known unit testing libraries—Jasmine.js.

2. Leverage the two way bindings and dependency tracking mechanism to test web applications using Knockout.js.

3. The book covers different JavaScript application testing strategies supported by real-world examples.

Building a Single Page Web Application with Knockout.js [Video]

ISBN: 978-1-78328-405-4   Duration: 01:51 hrs

Create a complete and structured single page application by doing more with less code using Knockout.js

1. Create a well-structured and organized application that you can build on and expand.

2. Learn how Knockout's data-binding can help you do more with less code.

3. Make use of best practices to ensure a maintainable code base.

Please check **www.PacktPub.com** for information on our titles

Printed in Great Britain
by Amazon.co.uk, Ltd.,
Marston Gate.